A Country Christmas

CONTENTS

INTRODUCTION

As we warm to the annual ritual of filling our kitchens with the homely smell of rich, spicy baking; as we welcome carol singers to the door with a glass of steaming hot mull, and gather the branches of evergreens to decorate our homes; as we write Christmas card messages to friends and relatives, and wrap presents for family and those we love; as we light candles, hang glittering ornaments on the tree and assemble for midnight mass; as we gather around the table for Christmas dinner, and later join in party games, we are carrying on traditions that have been perpetuated over two thousand years and have evolved, with remarkable similarities still, in many parts of the Christian world.

The festival of Christmas as it is celebrated today has its origins in pagan times, when ancient peoples throughout the northern hemisphere gathered together to feast and frolic at the winter solstice.

The transition from a string of pagan festivals to the festival of Christmas was gradual. In the early days of Christianity the birth of Christ was not only not celebrated, it was not even marked by a specific date. It was only in the fourth century that the church fixed the date of Christ's birth as December 25. Then, when St. Augustine arrived in Great Britain, he instructed the faithful to adopt many of the existing customs, applying new meanings and Christian standards to the ancient rituals. In that way, followers were not asked to forgo traditional pleasures.

In medieval Great Britain the emphasis fell heavily on the merrymaking aspect of the festival. Groups of masked mummers, usually men, performed plays in local villages and towns throughout England, receiving money, fruit and other seasonal foods in return for their entertainment. The plays usually centred on a fight between a hero and villain, with a quack doctor arriving in the nick of time to revive the fallen hero with magic potion.

With the rise of Puritanism in the seventeenth century, the merrymaking and, indeed, the celebration of Christmas had to stop. The Puritans denounced the festival and passed an Act of

Parliament prohibiting any celebrations, announcing that the only fitting way to commemorate the birth of Christ was to fast. They even employed troops to patrol the streets and ensure that no one broke the law and cooked lunch. In New England the Pilgrims and Puritans, in protest against what they saw as the laxity of the Church of England, refused to recognize Christmas Day as a holiday and eschewed all those customs with pagan origins.

With the restoration of the monarchy in Great Britain in 1660, Christmas feasting became increasingly lavish, and a journal of the time records that a London merchant's table was set with "... turkies, geese, capons, puddings  of a dozen sorts ... besides brawn, roast beef and many things ... minc'd pies and a thing called plumb pottage".

Although the turkey, after having been discovered in South America, had been brought to England in the sixteenth century, it did not become widely popular until the nineteenth century when Mrs Beeton, the Victorian writer on household management, pronounced it as "one of the most glorious presents made by the New World to the Old". It was in Victorian Great Britain that many existing Christmas customs were practised

with renewed enthusiasm, and many innovations were introduced, customs that are now deeply woven into the fabric of Christmas as it is celebrated today.

With marked lack of restraint, the Victorians covered their homes with evergreens, draping boughs across mirrors and picture frames, over mantels and furniture and weaving them in and out of the banisters. Those who could not gather greenery for themselves bought it from street vendors whose barrows were piled high with holly and mistletoe.

Then, in 1841, came the Christmas tree, which had played a prominent role in German festivities since the fifteenth century. When Queen Charlotte, wife of King George III, erected a tree at Windsor Castle in the late eighteenth century, its introduction had passed largely unnoticed. But

when Prince Albert, consort of Queen Victoria, reintroduced the custom, decorating the tree with glittering trinkets and baubles from his native Germany, it was as if everyone had been waiting for the moment. A photograph of the Royal Family

gathered around their tree appeared in a London journal and from then on a decorated and illuminated tree became the focal point of the festivities in Great Britain and, shortly afterwards, in the United States.

Although many tree decorations were made at home, manufacturers became more and more inventive, creating delicate and exquisite glass bells, balls, stars and other fancy, festive shapes, as well as twisted candles that fitted into "safety" holders.

The idea of decorating a tree with lighted candles is thought to have originated with Martin Luther, professor of theology at the Saxon University of Wittenburg in the early sixteenth century, as a way of reminding children that the birth of the infant Jesus brought light into the world. The first electric tree lights appeared in New York in 1882 when an associate of Thomas Edison used strings of coloured lights to illuminate his tree. A decade later, when they were manufactured commercially by The General Electric Company, this form of safety lighting became generally available.

The 1840s heralded the introduction to Victorian Great Britain not only of the Christmas tree,

but of Christmas cards and Christmas crackers as well. Christmas greetings cards evolved over several decades from an eighteenth-century school practice in Britain of writing "Christmas pieces", and the end-of-year reports presented by children to their parents to indicate what progress they had made at school. It was this custom, and the fact that the pieces became ever more elaborate, that prompted Henry (later Sir Henry) Cole, the first director of the Victoria & Albert Museum in London, to commission in 1843 the first known Christmas card. The hand-coloured and printed card, designed by his friend Sir John Callcot Horsley, R.A., showed a close family group seated at a table drinking red wine, and is flanked on either side by allegorical

sketches depicting kindly, charitable acts. Surrounded by a rustic vine entwined with ivy, a panel carries the seasonal message "A Merry Christmas and a Happy New Year to you".

Later designs depicted scenes of the typical Victorian Christmas: children dancing around a tree, gathering foliage, and playing games; families expressing delight at the entry of the Christmas pudding; skating on ponds, and playing with snowballs. The romantic idea of a white Christmas emanates from this time, a period of particularly harsh winters and deep snow, and has persisted long after the weather pattern has changed.

"Christmas won't be Christmas without presents" begins Louisa May Alcott's Victorian novel, *Little Women*, expressing a sentiment that would be echoed throughout the Christian world if Father Christmas, Santa Claus, St Nicholas, St Basil, Christkindl, La Befana, Grandfather Frost, Julenisse or any of the other benefactors were to fail in their customary distribution of gifts in December or January.

The familiar figure of Santa Claus or Father Christmas, red-robed, white-haired and jolly, has a somewhat confused ancestry. The distribution of gifts at that time of the year was part of many pagan rituals – Norsemen, for example, believed that their god Woden brought them gifts in honour of the winter solstice. And then, in the Christian church, a number of legends built up around St Nicholas, a fourth-century bishop of a Turkish See. He is said to have distributed baskets of grain, fruit and honey cakes to poor children, thrown bags of gold into a house where there were three young girls, and even brought back to life three boys who had been murdered. With so much good work to his credit, early churchmen conferred on St Nicholas the honour of being the distributor of Christmas gifts.

The legend of the bags of gold had far-reaching consequences. It is said that the gold landed in the girls' stockings which were hung up by the fire to dry, and this gave rise to the custom that is dear to children's hearts today. One of the traditional tokens placed in children's stockings, gold-wrapped chocolate coins, commemorates the wealthy prelate's gift. And the fact that the stockings were hung by the fire prompted St Nicholas – Father Christmas or Santa – to enter the house by the most direct route – down the chimney.

Originally the stockings hung up in eager anticipation would have been workaday ones, perhaps outgrown by the youngest child, but gradually they became an art form in themselves, ranging from those made of homespun check gingham cotton in the Shaker community of Pennsylvania – where sugar plums and molasses toffee were customary fillers – to the elaborate petit-point designs of the Victorians, where clove-studded oranges and nuts were obligatory gifts.

Festive Foods

TRADITIONAL
COOKING

In country communities all over the world,
families and friends gather to create
and share their own traditions. Here are
wholesome, failsafe recipes to ensure that
the heart of your festival glows with natural
warmth and goodwill.

Christmas Salad

A light first course that can be prepared ahead and assembled just before serving.

Serves 8

INGREDIENTS
mixed red and green lettuce leaves
2 sweet pink grapefruit
1 large or 2 small avocados, peeled
    and cubed

FOR THE DRESSING
90 ml/6 tbsp light olive oil
30 ml/2 tbsp red wine vinegar
1 garlic clove, crushed
5 ml/1 tsp Dijon mustard
salt and freshly ground black pepper

FOR THE CARAMELIZED ORANGE PEEL
4 oranges
50 g/2 oz/4 tbsp caster sugar
60 ml/4 tbsp cold water

lettuce leaves

red wine vinegar

oranges

avocados

grapefruit

olive oil

1 To make the caramelized peel, using a vegetable peeler, remove the rind from the oranges in thin strips and reserve the fruit. Scrape away the white pith from the underside of the rind with a sharp knife, and cut the rind in fine shreds.

2 Put the sugar and water in a small pan and heat gently until the sugar has dissolved. Then add the shreds of orange rind, increase the heat and boil steadily for 5 minutes, until the rind is tender. Using two forks, remove the orange rind from the syrup and spread it out on a wire rack to dry. (This can be done the day before.) Reserve the syrup to add to the dressing.

3 Wash and dry the lettuce and tear the leaves into bite-sized pieces. Wrap them in a clean, damp tea towel and keep them in the fridge. Cut the pith off the oranges and grapefruit. Holding the fruit over a bowl to catch any juice, cut them into segments, removing all the pith.

4 Put all the dressing ingredients into a screw-top jar and shake the jar vigorously to emulsify the dressing. Add the reserved orange-flavoured syrup and adjust the seasoning to taste. Arrange the salad ingredients on individual plates with the avocados, spoon over the dressing and scatter on the caramelized peel.

Warm Prawn Salad with Spicy Marinade

The ingredients can be prepared in advance; if you do this, cook the prawns and bacon just before serving, spoon over the salad and serve with hot herb and garlic bread.

Serves 8

INGREDIENTS
225 g/8 oz large, cooked, shelled
    prawns
225 g/8 oz smoked streaky bacon,
    chopped
mixed lettuce leaves
30 ml/2 tbsp snipped fresh chives

FOR THE LEMON AND CHILLI MARINADE
1 garlic clove, crushed
finely grated rind of 1 lemon
15 ml/1 tbsp lemon juice
60 ml/4 tbsp olive oil
¼ tsp chilli paste, or a large pinch
    dried ground chilli
15 ml/1 tbsp light soy sauce
salt and freshly ground black pepper

prawns
chilli paste
lettuce leaves
chives
soy sauce
lemon
garlic
bacon

1 In a glass bowl, mix the prawns with the garlic, lemon rind and juice, 45 ml/ 3 tbsp of oil, the chilli paste and soy sauce. Season with salt and pepper. Cover with clear film and leave to marinate for at least one hour.

2 Gently cook the bacon in the remaining oil until crisp. Drain on a kitchen towel.

3 Wash and dry the lettuce, tear the leaves into bite-sized pieces and arrange them in individual bowls or on plates.

4 Just before serving, put the prawns with their marinade into a large frying-pan, bring to the boil, add the bacon and cook for one minute. Spoon over the salad and sprinkle with snipped chives. Serve immediately.

Baked Gammon with Cumberland Sauce

Serve this delicious cooked meat and sauce either hot or cold. The gammon must be soaked overnight before cooking to remove any strong salty flavour resulting from the curing process.

Serves 8–10

INGREDIENTS
2.25 kg/5 lb smoked or unsmoked
   gammon joint
1 onion
1 carrot
1 celery stick
bouquet garni sachet
6 peppercorns

FOR THE GLAZE
whole cloves
2 oz/50 g/4 tbsp soft light brown or
   demerara sugar
30 ml/2 tbsp golden syrup
5 ml/1 tsp English mustard powder

FOR THE CUMBERLAND SAUCE
juice and shredded rind of 1 orange
30 ml/2 tbsp lemon juice
120 ml/4 fl oz/½ cup port or red wine
60 ml/4 tbsp redcurrant jelly

1 Soak the gammon overnight in a cool place in plenty of cold water to cover. Discard this water. Put the joint into a large pan and cover it again with more cold water. Bring the water to the boil slowly and skim any scum from the surface with a slotted spoon.

2 Add the vegetables and seasonings, cover and simmer very gently for 2 hours. (The meat can also be cooked in the oven at 180°C/350°F/Gas 4. Allow 30 minutes per 450 g/1 lb.)

3 Leave the meat to cool in the liquid for 30 minutes. Then remove it from the liquid and strip off the skin neatly with the help of a knife (use rubber gloves if the gammon is too hot to handle).

4 Score the fat in diamonds with a sharp knife and stick a clove in the centre of each diamond.

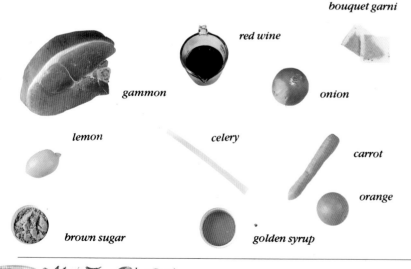

bouquet garni

red wine

gammon

onion

lemon

celery

carrot

orange

brown sugar

golden syrup

5 Preheat the oven to 180°C/350°F/ Gas 4. Put the sugar, golden syrup and mustard powder in a small pan and heat gently to melt them. Place the gammon in a roasting tin and spoon over the glaze. Bake it until golden brown, about 20 minutes. Put it under a hot grill, if necessary, to get a good colour. Allow to stand in a warm place for 15 minutes before carving (this allows the flesh to relax and makes carving much easier).

6 For the sauce, put the orange and lemon juice into a pan with the port and redcurrant jelly, and heat gently to melt the jelly. Pour boiling water on to the orange rind, drain, and add to the sauce. Cook gently for 2 minutes. Serve the sauce hot, in a sauce boat.

Roast Turkey

Serve with stuffing balls, bacon rolls, roast potatoes, Brussels sprouts and gravy.

Serves 8

INGREDIENTS

4.5 kg/10 lb oven-ready turkey, with giblets (thawed overnight if frozen)
1 large onion, peeled and stuck with 6 whole cloves
50 g/2 oz/4 tbsp butter, softened
10 chipolata sausages
salt and freshly ground black pepper

FOR THE STUFFING

225 g/8 oz rindless, streaky bacon, chopped
1 large onion, finely chopped
450 g/1 lb pork sausagemeat
25 g/1 oz/⅓ cup rolled oats
30 ml/2 tbsp chopped fresh parsley
10 ml/2 tsp dried mixed herbs
1 large egg, beaten
115 g/4 oz dried apricots, finely chopped

FOR THE GRAVY

25 g/1 oz/ 2 tbsp plain flour
450 ml/¾ pint/1⅞ cups giblet stock

bacon

turkey

onion

parsley

apricots   *oats*

1 Preheat the oven to 200°C/400°F/ Gas 6. Adjust the oven shelves to allow for the size of the turkey. For the stuffing, cook the bacon and onion gently in a pan until the bacon is crisp and the onion tender. Transfer to a large bowl and mix in all the remaining stuffing ingredients. Season well with salt and pepper.

4 Spread the turkey with the butter and season it with salt and pepper. Cover it loosely with foil and cook it for 30 minutes. Baste the turkey with the pan juices. Then lower the oven temperature to 180°C/350°F/Gas 4 and cook for the remainder of the calculated time (about 3½ hours for a 4.5 kg/10 lb bird). Baste it every 30 minutes or so.

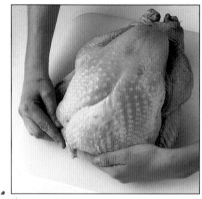

2 Stuff the neck-end of the turkey only, tuck the flap of skin under and secure it with a small skewer or stitch it with thread (do not over-stuff the turkey or the skin will burst during cooking). Reserve any remaining stuffing.

5 With wet hands, shape the remaining stuffing into small balls or pack it into a greased ovenproof dish. Cook in the oven for 20 minutes, or until golden brown and crisp. About 20 minutes before the end of cooking put the chipolata sausages into an ovenproof dish and put them in the oven. Remove the foil from the turkey for the last hour of cooking and baste it. The turkey is cooked if the juices run clear when the thickest part of the thigh has been pierced with a skewer.

3 Put the whole onion studded with cloves in the body cavity of the turkey and tie the legs together. Weigh the stuffed bird and calculate the cooking time; allow 15 minutes per 450 g/1 lb plus 15 minutes over. Place the turkey in a large roasting tin.

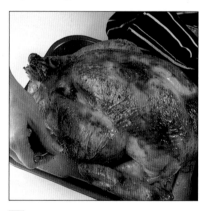

6 Transfer the turkey to a serving plate, cover it with foil and let it stand for 15 minutes before carving. To make the gravy, spoon off the fat from the roasting pan, leaving the meat juices. Blend in the flour and cook for 2 minutes. Gradually stir in the stock and bring to the boil. Check the seasoning and pour into a sauce boat. Remove the skewer or string and pour any juices into the gravy. To serve, surround the turkey with chipolata sausages, bacon rolls and stuffing balls.

Filo Vegetable Pie

This stunning pie makes a delicious main course for vegetarians or is an excellent accompaniment to cold sliced turkey or other meat dishes.

Serves 6–8

INGREDIENTS
225 g/8 oz leeks
165 g/5½ oz/11 tbsp butter
225 g/8 oz carrots, cubed
225 g/8 oz mushrooms, sliced
225 g/8 oz Brussels sprouts, quartered
2 garlic cloves, crushed
115 g/4 oz cream cheese
115 g/4 oz Roquefort or Stilton cheese
150 ml/¼ pint/⅔ cup double cream
2 eggs, beaten
225 g/8 oz cooking apples
225 g/8 oz/1 cup cashew nuts or pine nuts, toasted
350 g/12 oz frozen filo pastry, defrosted
salt and freshly ground black pepper

nuts
Brussels sprouts
Roquefort
carrots
apple
butter
leeks
eggs

1 Preheat the oven to 180°C/350°F/Gas 4. Cut the leeks in half through the root and wash them to remove any soil, separating the layers slightly to check they are clean. Slice into 1 cm/½ in pieces, drain and dry on kitchen paper.

2 Heat 40 g/1½ oz/3 tbsp of the butter in a large pan and cook the leeks and carrots covered over a medium heat for 5 minutes. Add the mushrooms, sprouts and garlic and cook for another 2 minutes. Turn the vegetables into a bowl and let them cool.

3 Whisk the cream cheese and blue cheese, cream, eggs and seasoning together in a bowl. Pour them over the vegetables. Peel and core the apples and cut into 1 cm/½ in cubes. Add them to the vegetables, with the toasted nuts.

4 Melt the remaining butter. Brush the inside of a 23 cm/9 in loose-based springform cake tin with melted butter. Brush two-thirds of the filo pastry sheets with butter, one at a time and use them to line the base and sides of the tin, overlapping the layers so that there are no gaps.

5 Spoon in the vegetable mixture and fold over the excess filo pastry to cover the filling.

6 Brush the remaining filo sheets with butter and cut them into 2.5 cm/1 in strips. Cover the top of the pie with these strips, arranging them in a rough mound. Bake for 35–45 minutes until golden brown all over. Allow to stand for 5 minutes, and then remove the cake tin and transfer to a serving plate.

Turkey and Cranberry Pie

The cranberries add a tart layer to this turkey pie. Cranberry sauce can be used if fresh cranberries are not available. The pie freezes well.

Serves 8

INGREDIENTS

450 g/1 lb pork sausagemeat
450 g/1 lb lean minced pork
15 ml/1 tbsp ground coriander
15 ml/1 tbsp dried mixed herbs
finely grated rind of 2 large oranges
10 ml/2 tsp grated fresh root ginger or
   2.5 ml/½ tsp ground ginger
10 ml/2 tsp salt
450 g/1 lb turkey breast fillets, thinly
   sliced
115 g/4 oz fresh cranberries
freshly ground black pepper

FOR THE PASTRY

450 g/1 lb/4 cups plain flour
5 ml/1 tsp salt
150 g/5 oz/⅔ cup lard
150 ml/¼ pint/⅔ cup mixed milk and
   water

TO FINISH

1 egg, beaten
300 ml/½ pint/1¼ cups aspic jelly,
   made up as packet instructions

cranberries

turkey fillets

pork

ginger

herbs

orange

coriander

1 Preheat the oven to 180°C/350°F/Gas 4. Place a baking tray in the oven to preheat. In a bowl, mix together the sausagemeat, pork, coriander, herbs, orange rind, ginger and salt and pepper.

2 To make the pastry, put the flour into a large bowl with the salt. Heat the lard in a small pan with the milk and water until just beginning to boil. Draw the pan aside and allow to cool slightly.

3 Using a wooden spoon, quickly stir the liquid into the flour until a very stiff dough is formed. Turn on to a work surface and knead until smooth. Cut one-third off the dough for the lid, wrap it in clear film and keep it in a warm place.

4 Roll out the large piece of dough on a floured surface and line the base and sides of a well-greased 20 cm/8 in loose-based, springform cake tin. Work with the dough while it is still warm, as it will crack and break if it is left to get cold.

5 Put the turkey breast fillets between two pieces of cling film and flatten with a rolling pin to a 3 mm/⅛ in thickness. Spoon half the pork mixture into the base of the tin, pressing it well into the edges. Cover with half of the turkey slices and then the cranberries, followed by the remaining turkey and finally the rest of the pork mixture.

6 Roll out the rest of the dough and cover the filling, trimming any excess and sealing the edges with a little beaten egg. Make a steam hole in the centre of the lid and decorate the top by cutting pastry trimmings into leaf shapes. Brush with beaten egg. Bake for 2 hours. Cover the pie with foil if the top gets too brown. Place the pie on a wire rack to cool. When cold, use a funnel to fill the pie with liquid aspic jelly. Leave to set for a few hours or overnight, before unmoulding the pie to serve it.

Brussels Sprouts with Chestnuts and Carrots

Be sure to allow plenty of time to peel the chestnuts; they are very fiddly but well worth the effort.

Serves 8

INGREDIENTS
450 g/1 lb fresh chestnuts
450 ml/¾ pint/1⅞ cups vegetable
  stock
450 g/1 lb Brussels sprouts
450 g/1 lb carrots
25 g/1 oz/2 tbsp butter
salt and freshly ground black pepper

carrots

butter

chestnuts

Brussels sprouts

1 Using a sharp knife, peel the raw chestnuts, leaving the brown papery skins intact. Bring a small pan of water to the boil, drop a handful of chestnuts into the water for a few minutes, and remove with a slotted spoon. The brown papery skins will slip off easily.

2 Put the peeled chestnuts in a pan with the stock. Cover the pan and bring to the boil. Simmer for 5–10 minutes, until tender. Drain.

3 Remove the outer leaves from the sprouts, if necessary, and trim the stalks level. Cook in a pan of boiling, salted water for about 5 minutes, or until just tender. Drain and rinse under cold running water to stop the cooking.

4 Peel the carrots and cut them in 1 cm/½ in diagonal slices. Put them in a pan with cold water to cover, bring to the boil and simmer until just tender, 5–6 minutes. Drain and rinse under cold running water. Melt the butter in a heavy-based pan, add the chestnuts, sprouts and carrots and season with salt and pepper. Cover with a lid and reheat, occasionally stirring the vegetables in the pan.

Sweet and Sour Red Cabbage

The cabbage can be cooked the day before and reheated for serving. It is a good accompaniment to goose, pork or strong-flavoured game dishes. The crispy bacon added at the end of cooking is optional and can be omitted.

Serves 8

INGREDIENTS
900 g/2 lb red cabbage
30 ml/2 tbsp olive oil
2 large onions, sliced
2 large cooking apples, peeled, cored and sliced
30 ml/2 tbsp cider vinegar
30 ml/2 tbsp soft brown sugar
225 g/8 oz rindless streaky bacon (optional)
salt and freshly ground black pepper

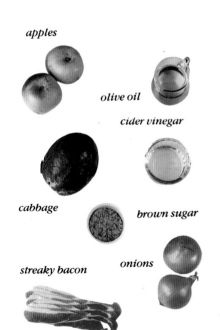

apples

olive oil

cider vinegar

cabbage

brown sugar

streaky bacon

onions

1 Preheat the oven to 180°C/350°F/Gas 4. Cut the cabbage into quarters through the stalk and shred it finely with a sharp knife or in a food processor, discarding the hard core.

2 Heat the oil in a large ovenproof casserole. Cook the onion over a gentle heat for 2 minutes.

3 Stir the cabbage, apples, vinegar, sugar and seasoning into the casserole. Cover with a tight-fitting lid and cook for about 1 hour, or until very tender. Stir half-way through cooking.

4 Chop the bacon, if using, and fry it gently in a pan until crisp. Stir it into the cabbage just before serving.

Carving a Turkey

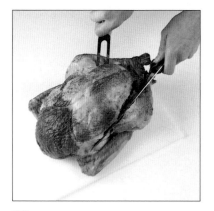

1 First remove the leg, by cutting the skin between the breast and leg. Press the leg flat, to expose the joint. Cut between the bones through the joint.

2 Cut the leg in two, through the joint.

3 Carve the leg into slices.

4 Remove the wing, cutting through the joint in the same way as for the leg.

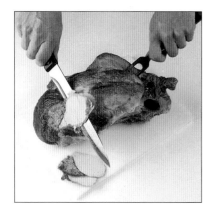

5 Carve the breast in thin slices, starting at the front of the breast. Then carve slices from the back of the breast, alternating the slices between front and back, until all the breast has been carved.

Times for Roasting Turkey

When choosing a turkey for Christmas, you should allow about 450 g/1 lb of dressed (plucked and oven-ready) bird per head. A good sized turkey to buy for Christmas is 4.5 kg/10 lb. This will serve about 12 people, with leftovers for the following day.

Thaw a frozen turkey, still in its bag, on a plate at room temperature (18–21°C/65–70°F) until the legs are flexible and there are no ice crystals in the cavity of the bird. Remove the giblets from the cavity as soon as the bird has thawed enough.

Oven-ready weight	Thawing time	Number of servings	Cooking time
3.5 kg/8 lb	18 hours	8–10 people	2½–3½ hours
4.5 kg/10 lb	19 hours	12–14 people	3½–4 hours
5.5 kg/12 lb	20 hours	16–18 people	3¾–4½ hours
6.3 kg/14 lb	24 hours	18–20 people	4–5 hours

These times apply to a turkey weighed after stuffing and at room temperature. Cook in a moderate oven, 180°C/350°F/Gas 4, covered with butter and bacon rashers and loosely covered with foil.

To test whether the turkey is fully cooked, push a skewer into the thickest part of the leg and press the flesh; the juices should run clear and free from any blood. The legs take longer than the breast to cook; keep the breast covered with foil until the legs are cooked. The foil can be removed for the final hour of cooking, to brown and crisp the skin. The turkey should be basted with the juices from the roasting tin, every hour of cooking.

Plan for the turkey to be ready 15–20 minutes before you want to serve dinner. Remove it from the oven and allow the flesh to relax before carving it.

Curried Fruit Chutney

Make this well ahead of Christmas, to serve with cold sliced turkey and ham.

Makes about 1.2 kg/2¹/₂ lb

INGREDIENTS
225 g/8 oz dried apricots
225 g/8 oz dried peaches
225 g/8 oz dates, stoned
225 g/8 oz/1¹/₃ cups raisins
1–2 garlic cloves, crushed
225 g/8 oz/1 generous cup soft light
   brown sugar
300 ml/¹/₂ pint/1¹/₄ cups white malt
   vinegar
300 ml/¹/₂ pint/1¹/₄ cups water
5 ml/1 tsp salt
10 ml/2 tsp mild curry powder

2 Chop or mince the mixture coarsely in batches in a food processor.

1 Put all the ingredients in a large pan, cover and simmer very gently for 10–15 minutes, or until tender.

3 Spoon into clean jam jars. Seal the jars and label them. Store in a cool place for 4 weeks before using.

Ginger, Date, and Apple Chutney

Make this well ahead and store it in airtight jars. Serve with cold sliced meats or pies.

Makes about 1.5 kg/3¹/₂ lb

INGREDIENTS
450 g/1 lb cooking apples
450 g/1 lb dates
225 g/8 oz dried apricots
115 g/4 oz glacé ginger, chopped
1–2 garlic cloves, crushed
225 g/8 oz/1¹/₃ cups sultanas
225 g/8 oz/1 generous cup soft light
   brown sugar
5 ml/1 tsp salt
300 ml/¹/₂ pint/1¹/₄ cups white malt
   vinegar

2 Put all the fruit together in a large pan, with the remaining ingredients. Cover and simmer gently for 10–15 minutes, or until tender.

1 Peel, core and chop the apples. Stone the dates and chop them roughly. Chop the apricots.

3 Spoon into clean jam jars. Seal the jars and label them. Store in a cool place for 4 weeks before using.

Prune, Orange and Nut Stuffing

You could also finely chop the reserved turkey liver and mix it into this stuffing.

Serves 8 (enough to stuff a 4.5 kg/10 lb turkey)

INGREDIENTS
115 g/4 oz/1 cup stoned prunes
60 ml/4 tbsp red wine or sherry
1 onion, finely chopped
25 g/1 oz/2 tbsp butter
225 g/8 oz/5 cups fresh white
    breadcrumbs
finely grated rind of 1 orange
2 eggs, beaten
30 ml/2 tbsp chopped fresh parsley
15 ml/1 tbsp mixed dried herbs
large pinch of ground allspice
large pinch of grated nutmeg
115 g/4 oz/1 cup chopped walnuts
    or pecans
2 celery sticks, finely chopped
salt and freshly ground black pepper

1 Put the prunes and red wine or sherry in a small pan, cover and simmer gently until tender. Set aside to cool.

2 Cook the onion gently in the butter until tender, about 10 minutes.

3 Cut each prune into four pieces. Mix all the ingredients in a large bowl and season well with salt and pepper.

Rice, Mushroom and Leek Stuffing

The rice gives this stuffing a crumbly, light texture.

Serves 8 (enough to stuff a 4.5 kg/10 lb turkey)

INGREDIENTS
115 g/4 oz/½ cup rice
25 g/1 oz/2 tbsp butter
225 g/8 oz leeks, washed and sliced
225 g/8 oz mushrooms, chopped
2 celery sticks, finely chopped
50 g/2 oz/½ cup chopped walnuts
1 egg, beaten
60 ml/4 tbsp chopped fresh parsley
10 ml/2 tsp dried thyme
finely grated rind of 1 lemon
225 g/8 oz apple, peeled, cored
    and diced
salt and freshly ground black pepper

2 Mix all the remaining ingredients thoroughly together in a large bowl and season with salt and pepper.

1 Cook the rice in plenty of boiling, salted water for 12 minutes until tender. Drain the rice thoroughly and let it cool. Melt the butter in a frying-pan and cook the leeks and mushrooms until tender. Increase the heat and cook to evaporate any remaining moisture in the pan. Set aside to cool.

3 Add the rice, and the leek and mushroom mixture to the bowl and mix together thoroughly.

Making Bacon Rolls

If you want to wrap stoned prunes or chicken livers inside each rasher cut the bacon rashers in half after stretching them.

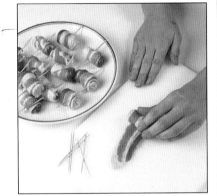

1 Remove the rind from the rashers of bacon and stretch them with the back of a large knife.

2 Roll the rashers up neatly.

3 Skewer the bacon rolls with cocktail sticks. Grill the rolls until crisp, turning them half-way through cooking.

Roasting Potatoes

Floury potatoes make the best crisp roast potatoes. Garlic or rosemary can be added to the oil, to flavour the potatoes during cooking.

1 Preheat the oven to 200°C/400°F/ Gas 6. Peel the potatoes and cut large potatoes in half. Parboil them for 10 minutes. Drain. Score the surface of each potato with a fork. Roll them in flour and tap them to remove any excess. Heat 2.5 cm/1 in olive oil in a shallow roasting tin until smoking hot.

2 Put the potatoes in the hot oil and baste them to coat them in oil. Roast for about an hour.

3 Baste and turn the potatoes twice during cooking. Drain them on kitchen paper and sprinkle them with salt.

CHRISTMAS CAKES
AND BAKES

These recipes for pudding, a classic cake,
a mince tart, a yule log, biscuits and
a country-style gingerbread house will
satisfy all your baking needs this
Christmas – for giving, entertaining or
treating your family.

Christmas Pudding

This recipe makes enough to fill one 1.2 litre/2 pint/ 5 cup basin or two 600 ml/1 pint/2½ cup basins. It can be made up to a month before Christmas and stored in a cool, dry place. Steam the pudding for 2 hours before serving. Serve with brandy or rum butter, whisky sauce, custard or whipped cream, topped with a decorative sprig of holly.

Serves 8

INGREDIENTS

115 g/4 oz/½ cup butter
225 g/8 oz/1 heaped cup soft dark
    brown sugar
50 g/2 oz/½ cup self-raising flour
5 ml/1 tsp ground mixed spice
¼ tsp grated nutmeg
2.5 ml/½ tsp ground cinnamon
2 eggs
115 g/4 oz/2 cups fresh white
    breadcrumbs
175 g/6 oz/1 cup sultanas
175 g/6 oz/1 cup raisins
115 g/4 oz/½ cup currants
25 g/1 oz/3 tbsp mixed candied peel,
    chopped finely
25 g/1 oz/¼ cup chopped almonds
1 small cooking apple, peeled, cored
    and coarsely grated
finely grated rind of 1 orange
    or lemon
juice of 1 orange or lemon, made up
    to 150 ml/¼ pint/⅔ cup with
    brandy, rum or sherry

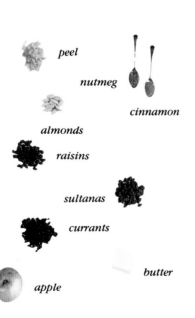

peel

nutmeg

cinnamon

almonds

breadcrumbs

raisins

sultanas

currants

brown sugar

orange

butter

apple

1 Cut a disc of greaseproof paper to fit the base of the basin(s) and butter the disc and basin(s).

2 Whisk the butter and sugar together until soft. Beat in the flour, spices and eggs. Stir in the remaining ingredients thoroughly. The mixture should have a soft dropping consistency.

3 Turn the mixture into the greased basin(s) and level the top.

4 Cover with another disc of buttered greaseproof paper.

5 Make a pleat across the centre of a large piece of greaseproof paper and cover the basin(s) with it, tying it in place with string under the rim. Cut off the excess paper. Pleat a piece of foil in the same way and cover the basin(s) with it, tucking it around the bowl neatly, under the greaseproof frill. Tie another piece of string around the basin(s) and across the top, as a handle.

6 Place the basin(s) in a steamer over a pan of simmering water and steam for 6 hours. Alternatively, put the basin(s) into a large pan and pour round enough boiling water to come halfway up the basin(s) and cover the pan with a tight-fitting lid. Check the water is simmering and top it up with boiling water as it evaporates. When the pudding(s) have cooked, leave to cool completely. Then remove the foil and greaseproof paper. Wipe the basin(s) clean and replace the greaseproof paper and foil with clean pieces, ready for reheating.

TO SERVE
Steam for 2 hours. Turn on to a plate and leave to stand for 5 minutes, before removing the pudding basin (the steam will rise to the top of the basin and help to loosen the pudding).

Moist and Rich Christmas Cake

The cake can be made 4–6 weeks before Christmas. During this time, pierce the cake with a fine needle and spoon over 30–45 ml/2–3 tbsp brandy.

Makes 1 cake

INGREDIENTS
225 g/8 oz/1⅓ cups sultanas
225 g/8 oz/1 cup currants
225 g/8 oz/1⅓ cups raisins
115 g/4 oz/1 cup prunes, stoned and chopped
50 g/2 oz/¼ cup glacé cherries, halved
50 g/2 oz/⅓ cup mixed candied citrus peel, chopped
45 ml/3 tbsp brandy or sherry
225 g/8 oz/2 cups plain flour
pinch of salt
2.5 ml/½ tsp ground cinnamon
2.5 ml/½ tsp grated nutmeg
15 ml/1 tbsp cocoa powder
225 g/8 oz/1 cup butter
225 g/8 oz/1 generous cup soft dark brown sugar
4 large eggs
finely grated rind of 1 orange or lemon
50 g/2 oz/⅔ cup ground almonds
50 g/2 oz/½ cup chopped almonds

TO DECORATE
60 ml/4 tbsp apricot jam
25 cm/10 in round cake board
450 g/1 lb almond paste
450 g/1 lb white fondant icing
225 g/8 oz royal icing
1½ m/1½ yd ribbon

raisins
flour
currants
almonds
butter
glacé cherries
prunes
nutmeg
cinnamon
cocoa powder
citrus peel

1 The day before you want to bake the cake, put all the dried fruit to soak in the brandy or sherry, cover it with clear film and leave overnight. Grease a 20 cm/8 in round cake tin and line it with a double thickness of greaseproof paper.

2 The next day, preheat the oven to 170°C/325°F/Gas 3. Sift together the flour, salt, spices and cocoa powder. Whisk the butter and sugar together until light and fluffy and beat in the eggs gradually. Finally mix in the orange or lemon rind, the ground and chopped almonds, dried fruits (with any liquid) and the flour mixture.

4 Warm then sieve the apricot jam to make a glaze. Remove the paper from the cake and place it in the centre of the cake board and brush it with hot apricot glaze. Cover the cake with a layer of almond paste and then a layer of fondant icing. Pipe a border around the base of the cake with royal icing. Tie a ribbon around the sides.

3 Spoon into the prepared cake tin, level the top and give the cake tin a gentle tap on the work surface to settle the mixture and disperse any air bubbles. Bake for 3 hours, or until a fine skewer inserted into the middle comes out clean. Transfer the cake tin to a wire rack and let the cake cool in the tin for an hour. Then carefully turn the cake out on to the wire rack, but leave the paper on, as it will help to keep the cake moist during storage. When the cake is cold, wrap it tightly in foil and store it in a cool place.

5 Roll out any trimmings from the fondant icing and stamp out 12 small holly leaves with a cutter. Make one bell motif with a biscuit mould, dusted first with sifted icing sugar. Roll 36 small balls for the holly berries. Leave on greaseproof paper to dry for 24 hours. Decorate the cake with the leaves, berries and bell, attaching them with a little royal icing.

Chocolate Christmas Log

Begin preparations for this cake at least one day ahead.
It is easy to prepare, but has several components.
Make the mushrooms by sandwiching small meringues
together with ganache frosting.

Serves 12–14

INGREDIENTS
5 eggs, separated
20 g/¾ oz/3 tbsp unsweetened cocoa
  plus extra for dusting
⅛ tsp cream of tartar
115 g/4 oz/1 cup icing sugar

CHOCOLATE GANACHE FROSTING
300 ml/10 fl oz/1¼ cups double or
  whipping cream
350 g/12 oz bittersweet chocolate,
  chopped
30 ml/2 tbsp brandy or chocolate-
  flavour liqueur

CRANBERRY CHRISTMAS SAUCE
450 g/1 lb fresh or frozen cranberries,
  rinsed and picked over
285 g/10 oz/1 cup seedless raspberry
  preserve, melted
100 g/3½ oz/½ cup granulated sugar,
  or to taste

WHITE CHOCOLATE CREAM FILLING
200 g/7 oz fine quality white
  chocolate, chopped
450 ml/16 fl oz/2 cups double cream
30 ml/2 tbsp brandy or chocolate-
  flavour liqueur (optional)

raspberry preserve

*bittersweet
chocolate*

cranberries

COOK'S TIP

Small decorative 'mushrooms' are
traditionally used to enhance the
chocolate yule log. These can be
made from meringue. Pipe the 'caps'
and 'stems' separately, and when dry
and hard, stick together using a little
ganache or melted chocolate. You
may lightly dust them with cocoa after
assembling.

1 Prepare ganache frosting. In a
medium saucepan over medium heat,
bring the cream to a boil. Remove from
heat and add chocolate all at once, stirring
constantly until melted and smooth. Stir in
liqueur if using, then strain into a medium
bowl and cool to room temperature.
Remove 125 ml/4 fl oz/½ cup at room
temperature, then refrigerate remaining
ganache for 6–8 hours or overnight.

2 Prepare sauce. In a food processor
fitted with a metal blade, process the
cranberries until liquid. Press through a
sieve into a small bowl, discard pulp. Stir
in melted raspberry preserve and sugar
to taste. If sauce is too thick, add a little
water to thin. Refrigerate until needed.

3 Prepare cake. Preheat oven to 200°C/
400°F/Gas 6. Grease 39 cm × 26 cm/15½
× 10½ in Swiss roll tin, line with non-stick
baking paper, overlapping edge by
2.5 cm/1 in.
  In a bowl with electric mixer, beat egg
yolks until thick and creamy. Reduce
speed and beat in cocoa and half the
sugar. In large bowl with electric mixer
with cleaned beaters, beat egg whites.
Add cream of tartar and beat on high
speed until soft peaks form. Add
remaining sugar 30 ml/2 tbsp at a time,
beating well after each addition until stiff
and glossy. Gently fold beaten yolk
mixture into the whites. Spread batter in
tin and bake for 15–20 minutes.
  Lay a clean dish towel on a work
surface and cover with non-stick baking
paper; dust with cocoa or sugar. When
cake is done, immediately turn out on to
paper. Peel off lining paper. Cut off crisp
edges and, starting from one narrow end,
roll cake with the paper and towel, Swiss
roll fashion. Cool cake.

4 Prepare filling. In a saucepan over low heat, melt white chocolate with 125 ml/4 fl oz/½ cup cream until melted, stirring frequently. Strain into a bowl and cool to room temperature. In another bowl with electric mixer, beat remaining cream and brandy until soft peaks form. Stir a spoonful of cream into white chocolate mixture to lighten it, then fold in remaining cream. Unroll cooled cake and spread with chocolate cream. Starting from the same end, re-roll cake without paper (it doesn't matter if it cracks). Cut off one-quarter at an angle. Place against the long piece to resemble a branch.

5 Allow frosting to soften at room temperature. With an electric mixer, beat the ganache until it begins to lighten in colour and texture, about 30–45 seconds. It should have a soft spreading consistency; do not over-beat as chocolate will become stiff and grainy. Using a metal palette knife, spread ganache over the cake surface. Using a fork, mark the ganache lengthwise to resemble tree bark. Dust cake with icing sugar and serve with cranberry sauce.

De Luxe Mincemeat Tart

The mincemeat can be made up and kept in the fridge for up to two weeks. It can also be used to make individual mince pies.

Serves 8

INGREDIENTS

225 g/8 oz/2 cups plain flour
10 ml/2 tsp ground cinnamon
50 g/2 oz/⅔ cup walnuts, finely ground
115 g/4 oz/½ cup butter
50 g/2 oz/4 tbsp caster sugar, plus
    extra for dusting
1 egg
2 drops vanilla essence
15 ml/1 tbsp cold water

FOR THE MINCEMEAT

2 dessert apples, peeled, cored and
    coarsely grated
225 g/8 oz/1⅓ cups raisins
115 g/4 oz no-soak dried apricots,
    chopped
115 g/4 oz no-soak dried figs or
    prunes, chopped
225 g/8 oz green grapes, halved and
    seeded
50 g/2 oz/½ cup chopped almonds
finely grated rind of 1 lemon
30 ml/2 tbsp lemon juice
30 ml/2 tbsp brandy or port
¼ tsp ground mixed spice
115 g/4 oz/generous ½ cup soft light
    brown sugar
25 g/1 oz/2 tbsp butter, melted

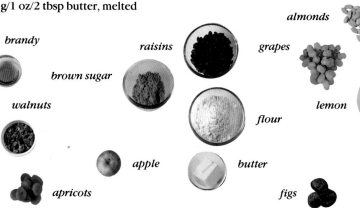

2 Mix all the mincemeat ingredients together thoroughly in a bowl.

1 To make the pastry, put the flour, cinnamon and walnuts in a food processor. Add the butter and process until the mixture resembles fine breadcrumbs. Turn into a bowl and stir in the sugar. Using a fork, beat the egg with the vanilla essence and water. Gradually stir the egg mixture into the dry ingredients. Gather together with your fingertips to form a soft, pliable dough. Knead briefly on a lightly floured surface until smooth; then wrap the dough in clear film and chill it for 30 minutes.

3 Cut one-third off the pastry and reserve it for the lattice. Roll out the remainder and use it to line a 23 cm/9 in, loose-based flan tin. Take care to push the pastry well into the edges and make a 5 mm/¼ in rim around the top edge.

4 With a rolling pin, roll off the excess pastry to neaten the edge. Fill the pastry case with the mincemeat.

almonds
brandy
raisins
grapes
brown sugar
walnuts
lemon
flour
apple
butter
apricots
figs

5 Roll out the remaining pastry and cut it into 1 cm/½ in strips. Arrange the strips in a lattice over the top of the pastry, wet the joins and press them together well. Chill for 30 minutes.

6 Preheat the oven to 190°C/375°F/ Gas 5. Place a baking sheet in the oven to preheat. Brush the pastry with water and dust it with caster sugar. Bake it on the baking sheet for 30–40 minutes. Transfer to a wire rack and leave to cool for 15 minutes. Then carefully remove the flan tin. Serve warm or cold, with sweetened, whipped cream.

Christmas Biscuits

These are great fun for children to make as presents. Any shape of biscuit cutter can be used. Store them in an airtight tin. For a change, omit the lemon rind and add 25 g/1 oz/⅓ cup of ground almonds and a few drops of almond essence.

Makes about 12

INGREDIENTS
75 g/3 oz/6 tbsp butter
50 g/2 oz/generous ½ cup icing sugar
finely grated rind of 1 small lemon
1 egg yolk
175 g/6 oz/1½ cups plain flour
pinch of salt

TO DECORATE
2 egg yolks
red and green edible food colouring

1 In a large bowl, beat the butter, sugar and lemon rind together until pale and fluffy. Beat in the egg yolk, and then sift in the flour and the salt. Knead together to form a smooth dough. Wrap in clear film and chill for 30 minutes.

2 Preheat the oven to 190°C/375°F/ Gas 5. On a lightly floured surface, roll out the dough to 3 mm/⅛ in thick. Using a 6 cm/2½ in fluted cutter, stamp out as many biscuits as you can, with the cutter dipped in flour to prevent it from sticking to the dough.

3 Transfer the biscuits on to lightly greased baking trays. Mark the tops lightly with a 2.5 cm/1 in holly leaf cutter and use a 5 mm/¼ in plain piping nozzle for the berries. Chill for 10 minutes, until firm.

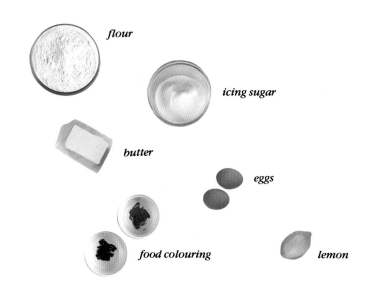

flour

icing sugar

butter

eggs

food colouring   lemon

4 Meanwhile, put each egg yolk into a small cup. Mix red food colouring into one and green food colouring into the other. Using a small, clean paintbrush, carefully paint the colours on to the biscuits. Bake the biscuits for 10–12 minutes, or until they begin to colour around the edges. Let them cool slightly on the baking trays, and then transfer them to a wire rack to cool completely.

Gingerbread House

This gingerbread house makes a memorable family gift, especially if filled with lots of little gifts and surprises.

Makes 1

INGREDIENTS
90 ml/6 tbsp golden syrup
30 ml/2 tbsp black treacle
75 g/3 oz/⅓ cup light soft brown sugar
75 g/3 oz/5 tbsp butter
450 g/1 lb/4 cups plain flour
15 g/1 tbsp ground ginger
15 g/1 tbsp bicarbonate of soda
2 egg yolks
225 g/8 oz barley sugar sweets

ICING AND DECORATION
1 quantity royal icing
25 cm/10 in square silver cake board

black treacle

biscuit cutters

barley sugar sweets

eggs

golden syrup

ROYAL ICING (enough to cover a 20 cm/8 in round cake)

Beat 2 egg whites in a bowl with 5 ml/1 tsp lemon juice. Sift in 450 g/1 lb icing sugar, a little at a time, until stiff peaks form. Cover until needed.

1 Preheat the oven to 190°C/375°F/Gas 5. Line several baking sheets with non-stick baking paper. Cut out the templates. Place the syrup, treacle, sugar and butter in a saucepan and heat gently, stirring occasionally until melted.

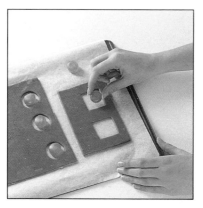

4 Repeat the above instructions using the remaining dough for the 2 side walls and the two roof pieces. Using the 2.5 cm/1 in square cutter, stamp out 2 window shapes for each wall piece. Using the 2.5 cm/1 in round cutter, stamp out 3 round windows on each roof piece. Place sweets in the openings and bake as before.

2 Sift the flour, ginger and bicarbonate of soda into a bowl. Add the egg yolks and pour in the treacle mixture, stirring with a wooden spoon to form a soft dough. Knead on a lightly floured surface until smooth and place in a polythene bag. Cut off ⅓ of the dough and roll out thinly.

3 Place the template for the end walls at one end and cut neatly around the shape using a sharp knife. Repeat to cut another end wall. Using a 2.5 cm/1 in round cutter, stamp out 1 round window on each end piece. Cut a door shape on each end piece using a 2.5 cm/1 in square cutter and rounding off the tops. Place a sweet in each opening and bake in the oven for 8–10 minutes until the sweet has filled the frame and the gingerbread is golden. Cool on the baking sheet.

5 Make the royal icing. Place some of the icing in a greaseproof paper piping bag fitted with a No. 2 plain writing nozzle. Pipe lines, loops and circles around the windows, doors and on the walls and roof to decorate. Pipe beads of icing in groups of 3 all over the remaining spaces and leave flat to dry.

TEMPLATES FOR THE GINGERBREAD HOUSE

1 For the side wall, measure and cut out a rectangle 15 cm × 10 cm (6 in × 4 in) from stiff card.

2 For the pitch of the roof, measure and cut out a rectangle 18 cm × 10 cm (7 in × 4 in). Measure 10 cm (4 in) up each long side and mark these points. Mark a centre point at the top of the short edge. Draw a line from each of the side points to the top point. Cut out.

3 For the roof, measure and cut out a rectangle 20 cm × 10 cm (8 in × 6 in) from stiff card.

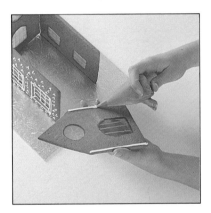

6 To assemble the house, pipe a line of icing on the side edges of the walls and side pieces. Stick them together to form a box shape on the cake board. Pipe a line of icing following the pitch of the roof on both end pieces and along the top of the 2 roof pieces. Press gently in position and support the underneath of each roof while the icing sets. Pipe the finishing touches to the roof and base of the house. Dust the cake board with icing sugar to look like snow. Wrap ribbon around the edges of the board.

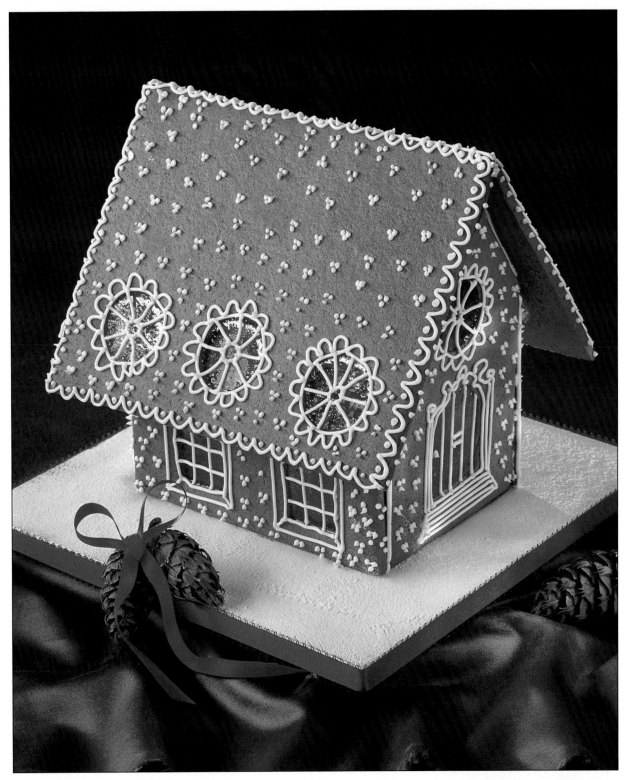

CHRISTMAS TREATS

Delight visitors, friends and family with
these really special indulgences – individual
ideas that reflect the thoughts and feelings
you have for your loved ones.

Festive Gingerbread

These brightly decorated gingerbread biscuits are fun to make and may be used as edible Christmas tree decorations.

Makes 20

INGREDIENTS
30 ml/2 tbsp golden syrup
15 ml/1 tbsp black treacle
50 g/2 oz/¼ cup light soft brown
 sugar
25 g/1 oz/2 tbsp butter
175 g/6 oz/1½ cups plain flour
¾ tsp bicarbonate of soda
½ tsp ground mixed spice
1½ tsp ground ginger
1 egg yolk

ICING AND DECORATION
½ quantity royal icing
red, yellow and green food colourings
brightly coloured ribbons

biscuit cutters

ginger

egg

1 Preheat the oven to 190°C/375°F/ Gas 5. Line several baking sheets with non-stick baking paper. Place the syrup, treacle, sugar and butter into a saucepan. Heat gently, stirring occasionally, until the butter has melted.

2 Sift the flour, bicarbonate of soda, mixed spice and ginger into a bowl. Using a wooden spoon stir in the treacle mixture and the egg yolk and mix to a soft dough. Knead on a lightly floured surface until smooth.

3 Roll out the dough thinly and, using a selection of festive cutters, stamp out as many shapes as possible, kneading and re-rolling the dough as necessary. Arrange the shapes well spaced apart on the baking sheets. Make a hole in the top of each shape using a drinking straw if you wish to use the biscuits as hanging decorations.

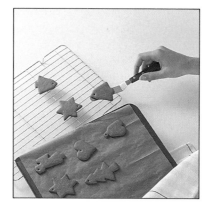

ROYAL ICING (enough to cover a 20 cm/8 in round cake) Beat 2 egg whites in a bowl with 5 ml/1 tsp lemon juice. Sift in 450 g/ 1 lb icing sugar, a little at a time, until stiff peaks form. Cover until needed.

4 Bake in the oven for 15–20 minutes or until risen and golden and leave to cool on the baking sheets before transferring to a wire rack using a palette knife.

5 Divide the royal icing into 4 and colour ¼ red, ¼ yellow and ¼ green using the food colourings. Make 4 greaseproof paper piping bags and fill each one with the different coloured icings. Fold down the tops and snip off the points.

6 Pipe lines, dots, and zigzags on the gingerbread biscuits using the coloured icings. Leave to dry. Thread ribbons through the holes in the biscuits.

Hogmanay Shortbread

Light, crisp shortbread looks so professional when shaped in a mould, although you could also shape it by hand.

Makes 2 large or 8 individual shortbreads

INGREDIENTS
175 g/6 oz/¾ cup plain flour
50 g/2 oz/¼ cup cornflour
50 g/2 oz/¼ cup caster sugar
115 g/4 oz/½ cup unsalted butter

flour

sugar

butter

1 Preheat the oven to 160°C/325°F/ Gas 3. Lightly flour the mould and line a baking sheet with non-stick baking paper. Sift the flour, cornflour and sugar into a mixing bowl. Cut the butter into pieces and rub into the flour mixture until it binds together and you can knead it into a soft dough.

2 Place the dough into the mould and press to fit neatly. Invert the mould onto the baking sheet and tap firmly to release the dough shape. Bake in the oven for 35–40 minutes or until pale golden.

3 Sprinkle the top of the shortbread with a little caster sugar and cool on the baking sheet. Wrap in cellophane paper or place in a box tied with ribbon.

Christmas Tree Biscuits

These biscuits make an appealing gift. They look wonderful hung on a Christmas tree or in front of a window to catch the light.

Makes 12

INGREDIENTS
175 g/6 oz/1½ cups plain flour
75 g/3 oz/5 tbsp butter
40 g/1½ oz/3 tbsp caster sugar
1 egg white
30 ml/2 tbsp orange juice
225 g/8 oz coloured fruit sweets

DECORATION
coloured ribbons

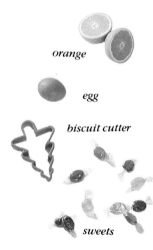

orange

egg

biscuit cutter

sweets

1 Preheat the oven to 180°C/350°F/ Gas 4. Line 2 baking sheets with non-stick baking paper. Sift the flour into a mixing bowl. Cut the butter into pieces and rub into the flour until the mixture resembles fine breadcrumbs. Stir in the sugar, egg white and enough orange juice to form a soft dough. Knead on a lightly floured surface until smooth.

2 Roll out thinly and stamp out as many shapes as possible using a Christmas tree cutter. Transfer the shapes to the lined baking sheets well spaced apart. Knead the trimmings together. Using a 1 cm/½ in round cutter or the end of a plain meringue piping nozzle, stamp out and remove 6 rounds from each tree shape. Cut each sweet into 3 and place a piece in each hole. Make a small hole at the top of each tree to thread through the ribbon.

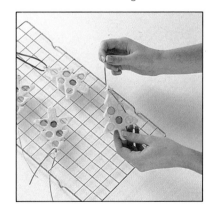

3 Bake in the oven for 15–20 minutes, until the biscuits are slightly gold in colour and the sweets have melted and filled the holes. Cool on the baking sheets. Repeat until you have used up the remaining biscuit dough and sweets. Thread short lengths of ribbon through the holes so that you can hang up the biscuits.

Mini Iced Christmas Cakes

A personal Christmas cake makes an extra special gift. Try improvising with your own designs, decorations and colour schemes.

Makes 1 large or 4 individual cakes

Ingredients

350 g/12 oz/1½ cups mixed dried fruit
50 g/2 oz/¼ cup glacé cherries, sliced
50 g/2 oz/½ cup flaked almonds
grated rind of ½ lemon
15 ml/1 tbsp brandy
115 g/4 oz/1 cup plain flour
½ tsp ground mixed spice
25 g/1 oz/⅓ cup ground almonds
90 g/3½ oz/½ cup unsalted butter, softened
90 g/3½ oz/½ cup dark soft brown sugar
½ tbsp black treacle
2 eggs

Icing and Decoration

4 × 10 cm/4 in square cake boards
60 ml/4 tbsp apricot glaze
675 g/1½ lb white marzipan
900 g/2 lb ready-to-roll icing
red and green food colourings

lemon

glacé cherries

almonds

marzipan

1 Prepare a 15 cm/6 in square cake tin. Place the mixed dried fruit, cherries, flaked almonds, lemon rind and brandy into a large mixing bowl. Stir until thoroughly blended, cover with clear film and leave for 1 hour or overnight.

2 Preheat the oven to 150°C/300°F/ Gas 2. Sift the flour and mixed spice into another bowl, add the ground almonds, butter, sugar, treacle and eggs. Mix together with a wooden spoon and beat for 2–3 minutes until smooth and glossy. Alternatively use a food mixer or processor for 1 minute. Fold the fruit into the cake mixture until evenly blended. Place the mixture in the prepared tin, level the top and make a slight depression in the centre.

3 Bake the cake in the centre of the oven for 2¼–2½ hours or until a skewer inserted into the centre of the cake comes out clean. Leave the cake to cool in the tin. Spoon over a little extra brandy if desired. Remove the cake from the tin and wrap in foil until required.

4 Remove the lining paper and cut the cake into 4 square pieces. Place each cake on a small cake board and brush evenly with apricot glaze. Cut the marzipan into 4 pieces and roll out a piece large enough to cover one cake. Place over the cake, smooth over the top and sides and trim off the excess marzipan at the base. Repeat to cover the remaining 3 cakes.

Apricot Glaze

Heat apricot jam with a squeeze of lemon juice in a pan until just melted. Strain, then return to the pan. Keep the glaze warm and brush generously over the cake.

5 Cut the ready-to-roll icing into 5 pieces, roll 4 pieces out thinly to cover each cake, smoothing the tops and sides and trimming off the excess icing at the bases. Knead the trimmings together with the remaining piece of icing and cut into 2 pieces. Colour one piece red and the other piece green using the food colourings. Roll out ½ of the red icing into a 25 × 15 cm/10 × 6 in oblong.

6 Cut the icing into 5 mm/¼ in strips and place diagonally across the cake working from corner to corner. Trim the strips at the base of the cake. Brush the ends of the strips with a little water and press onto the cake. Make a few loops of icing and place on top of the cake. Repeat to decorate the remaining cakes with green and finally red and green strips of icing. Pack into boxes when dry.

Individual Dundee Cakes

Dundee cakes are traditionally topped with almonds but also look tempting covered with glacé fruits.

Makes 3

INGREDIENTS
225 g/8 oz/1 cup raisins
225 g/8 oz/1 cup currants
225 g/8 oz/1 cup sultanas
50 g/2 oz/¼ cup glacé cherries, sliced
115 g/4 oz/¾ cup mixed peel
grated rind of 1 orange
300 g/11 oz/2¾ cups plain flour
½ tsp baking powder
5 g/1 tsp ground mixed spice
225 g/8 oz/1 cup unsalted butter, softened
225 g/8 oz/1 cup caster sugar
5 eggs

TOPPING
50 g/2 oz/½ cup whole blanched almonds
50 g/2 oz/¼ cup glacé cherries, halved
50 g/2 oz/½ cup glacé fruits, sliced
45 ml/3 tbsp Apricot Glaze

orange

glacé cherries

almonds

peel

egg

glacé fruits

1 Preheat the oven to 150°C/300°F/ Gas 2. Prepare 3 × 15 cm/5 in round cake tins. Place all the fruit and the orange rind into a large mixing bowl. Mix together until evenly blended. In another bowl sift the flour, baking powder and mixed spice. Add the butter, sugar and eggs. Mix together with a wooden spoon and beat for 2–3 minutes until smooth and glossy. Alternatively use a food mixer or processor for 1 minute.

2 Add the mixed fruit to the cake mixture and fold in using a spatula until well blended. Divide the cake mixture between the 3 tins and level the tops. Arrange the almonds in circles over the top of one cake, the glacé cherries over the second cake and the mixed glacé fruits over the last one. Bake in the oven for approximately 2–2½ hours or until a skewer inserted into the centre of the cakes comes out clean.

3 Leave the cakes in their tins until completely cold. Turn out, remove the paper and brush the tops with Apricot Glaze. Leave to set, then wrap in cellophane paper or clear film and place in pretty boxes.

Spiced Christmas Cake

This light cake mixture is flavoured with spices and fruit. It can be served with a dusting of icing sugar and decorated with holly leaves.

Makes 1

INGREDIENTS
225 g/8 oz/1 cup butter, plus extra for greasing
15 g/1 tbsp fresh white breadcrumbs
225 g/8 oz/1 cup caster sugar
50 ml/2 fl oz/¼ cup water
3 eggs, separated
225 g/8 oz/2 cups self-raising flour
7.5 g/1½ tsp ground mixed spice
25 g/1 oz/2 tbsp chopped angelica
25 g/1 oz/2 tbsp mixed peel
50 g/2 oz/¼ cup glacé cherries, chopped
50 g/2 oz/½ cup walnuts, chopped
icing sugar, to dust

1 Preheat the oven to 180°C/350°F/ Gas 4. Brush a 20 cm/8 in, 1.5 litre/ 2½ pint fluted ring mould with melted butter and coat with breadcrumbs, shaking out any excess.

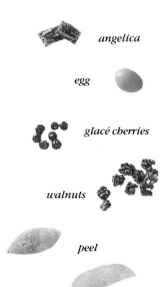

angelica

egg

glacé cherries

walnuts

peel

2 Place the butter, sugar and water into a saucepan. Heat gently, stirring occasionally, until melted. Boil for 3 minutes until syrupy, then allow to cool. Place the egg whites in a clean bowl, whisk until stiff. Sift the flour and spice into a bowl, add the angelica, mixed peel, cherries and walnuts and stir well to mix. Add the egg yolks.

3 Pour the cooled mixture into the bowl and beat together with a wooden spoon to form a soft batter. Gradually fold in the egg whites using a plastic spatula until the mixture is evenly blended. Pour into the prepared mould and bake for 50–60 minutes or until the cake springs back when pressed in the centre. Turn out and cool on a wire rack. Dust thickly with icing sugar and decorate with a sprig of holly.

PARTY FOOD
& DRINK

Whether you are planning an extravagant
party for the hungry hordes or a quiet get
together for a few close friends, these simple
snacks will ensure a relaxing and successful
time for you and a filling and delicious
meal for your guests. Providing unusual
drinks helps make Christmas different and
special; the following nine drinks ideas show you
how to create the tastes, spicy flavours
and warming atmosphere of a traditional
country festival.

Corn Muffins with Ham

These delicious little muffins are simple to make. If you like, serve them unfilled with a pot of herb butter.

Makes 24

INGREDIENTS
60 g/2 oz/scant ½ cup yellow cornmeal
70 g/2½ oz/⅔ cup plain flour
30 ml/2 tbsp sugar
7.5 ml/1½ tsp baking powder
2.5 ml/½ tsp salt
60 g/2 oz/4 tbsp butter, melted
120 ml/4 fl oz/½ cup whipping cream
1 egg, beaten
1–2 jalapeño or other medium-hot chillies, seeded and finely chopped (optional)
pinch cayenne pepper
butter, for spreading
grainy mustard or mustard with honey, for spreading
60 g/2 oz oak-smoked ham

whipping cream

plain flour

ham

sugar

grainy mustard

cornmeal

cayenne pepper

egg

baking powder

jalapeño chillies

butter

1 Preheat the oven to 200°C/400°F/Gas 6 and lightly grease a mini muffin pan with 24 4 cm/1½ in cups. In a large bowl combine the cornmeal, flour, sugar, baking powder and salt. In another bowl, whisk together the melted butter, cream, beaten egg, chopped chillies, if using, and the cayenne pepper.

2 Make a well in the cornmeal mixture, pour in the egg mixture and gently stir into the dry ingredients just enough to blend (do not over-beat – the batter does not have to be smooth).

3 Drop 15 ml/1 tbsp batter into each muffin cup and bake for 12–15 minutes, until golden and just firm to the touch. Remove the tray to a wire rack to cool slightly, then turn out the muffins on to the rack, and leave to cool completely.

4 With a sharp knife, split the muffins and spread each bottom half with a little butter and mustard. Cut out small rounds of ham with a round pastry cutter or cut into small squares, and place on the buttered muffins. Sandwich together each muffin with its top and serve.

COOK'S TIP
Muffins can be made in advance and stored in air-tight containers. Bring to room temperature or warm slightly before filling and serving.

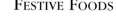

Tortelloni Kebabs

This hors d'oeuvre is easy to make and always popular. Any favourite dipping sauce can be substituted, or just drizzle the kebabs with good virgin olive oil and sprinkle with freshly grated Parmesan.

Makes about 64

INGREDIENTS
450 g/1 lb fresh cheese-filled
   tortelloni
10 ml/2 tsp olive oil
basil leaves, to garnish

FOR THE SAUCE
1 × 450 g/16 oz jar roasted red
   peppers, drained
1 garlic clove, chopped
15 ml/1 tbsp olive oil
15 ml/1 tbsp balsamic vinegar
5 ml/1 tsp sugar
freshly ground black pepper
2–3 dashes hot pepper sauce

garlic

*roasted
red pepper*

olive oil

tortelloni

hot pepper sauce

basil

sugar

*balsamic
vinegar*

1 Put the ingredients for the sauce into the bowl of a food processor and process until smooth, scraping down the sides once or twice. Sieve into a serving bowl and cover until ready to serve.

2 Bring a large saucepan of lightly salted water to a fast boil. Add the tortelloni and cook according to the instructions on the packet, for 8–10 minutes. Drain, rinse in warm water and turn into a bowl. Toss with olive oil to prevent sticking. Cover until ready to serve.

3 Using small, 15 cm/6 in wooden skewers, thread a basil leaf and 1 tortelloni on to each skewer. Arrange on a plate and serve warm, or at room temperature with the dipping sauce.

COOK'S TIP
The sauce can be made up to a day in advance or frozen for several weeks.

Celery Sticks with Roquefort

This delicious filling can also be made with English Stilton or any other blue cheese. Diluted with a little milk or cream, it also makes a delicious dip.

Makes about 45

INGREDIENTS
200 g/7 oz Roquefort or other blue
    cheese, softened
275 g/10 oz/1¼ cups lowfat cream
    cheese
2 green onions, finely chopped
black pepper
5–10 ml/1–2 tsp milk
1 celery head
chopped walnuts or hazelnuts, to
    garnish

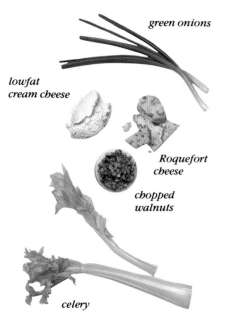

green onions

*lowfat
cream cheese*

*Roquefort
cheese*

*chopped
walnuts*

celery

1 With a fork, crumble the Roquefort in a bowl. Put in a food processor with the cream cheese, green onions, and black pepper. Process until smooth, scraping down the side of the bowl once or twice and gradually adding milk if the mixture seems too stiff.

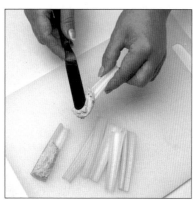

2 If you like, peel the celery lightly to remove any heavy strings before cutting each stalk into 3- to 4-inch pieces. Using a small knife, fill each celery stick with a little cheese mixture and press on a few chopped nuts. Arrange on a serving plate and refrigerate until ready to serve.

COOK'S TIP

For a more elegant presentation, fill a pastry bag fitted with a small star tip with the cheese mixture and carefully pipe mixture into the celery sticks. Press on the nuts.

Italian-style Marinated Artichokes

Good-quality extra-virgin olive oil together with fresh herbs turn canned or frozen artichoke hearts into a delicious snack.

Makes about 750 ml/1¼ pints/3 cups

INGREDIENTS
2 x 400 g/14 oz cans artichoke hearts
    in salt water
175 ml/6 fl oz/¾ cup extra-virgin
    olive oil
5 ml/1 tsp chopped fresh thyme, or
    2.5 ml/½ tsp dried thyme
5 ml/1 tsp chopped fresh oregano or
    marjoram, or 2.5 ml/½ tsp dried
    oregano or marjoram
2.5 ml/½ tsp fennel seeds, lightly
    crushed
1–2 garlic cloves, finely chopped
freshly ground black pepper
grated peel and juice of ½ lemon

thyme

*artichoke
hearts*

lemon

black pepper

oregano

lemon peel

*extra-virgin
olive oil*

fennel seeds

1 Rinse the artichokes, then drain them on paper towels. Cut any large ones in half lengthways.

2 Put the artichokes in a large saucepan with the next six ingredients, stir to combine, then cook, covered, over very low heat for 8 to 10 minutes until the flavours infuse. Remove from the heat and leave to cool slightly, then gently stir in the lemon peel and juice. Refrigerate. Return to room temperature before serving on toothpicks.

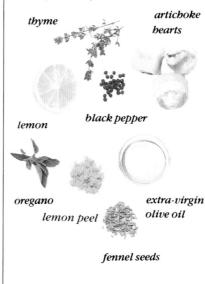

Mini Jacket Potatoes with Sour Cream and Chives

Jacket potatoes are always delicious, and the toppings can easily be varied – from caviar and smoked salmon to cheese and baked beans.

Makes 36

INGREDIENTS
36 potatoes, about 4 cm/1½ in
 in diameter, well scrubbed
250 ml/8 fl oz/1 cup thick sour cream
45–60 ml/3–4 tbsp snipped fresh
 chives
coarse salt, for sprinkling

sour cream

potatoes

chives

1 Preheat the oven to 180°C/350°F/ Gas 4. Place potatoes on a baking sheet and bake for 30–35 minutes, or until tender when pierced with the tip of a knife.

2 To serve, make a cross in the top of each potato and squeeze gently to open. Using the handle of a wooden spoon, make a hole in the centre of each potato. Fill each hole with a little sour cream, then sprinkle with the salt and the chives. Serve immediately, or at room temperature.

VARIATION

If your guests are likely to be hungry, use medium size potatoes. When cooked, cut in half, scoop out the flesh, mash with the other ingredients and spoon the mixture back into the skin. Serve warm.

COOK'S TIP

The potatoes can be baked in advance, then reheated in the microwave on High (100%) for 3–4 minutes.

Savoury Cheese Balls

These colourful little cheese balls are made in four different flavours, each variety coated with a different herb or seed.

Makes about 48

INGREDIENTS

450 g/1 lb/2⅔ cups cream cheese at
   room temperature
25 g/1 oz/¼ cup grated mature
   Cheddar cheese
2.5 ml/½ tsp dry mustard powder,
   prepared
5 ml/1 tsp mango chutney, chopped
   (optional)
cayenne pepper
salt
50 g/2 oz Roquefort or Stilton cheese
15 ml/1 tbsp finely chopped spring
   onions or snipped fresh chives
5–10 ml/1–2 tsp bottled pesto sauce
15 ml/1 tbsp chopped pine nuts
1–2 garlic cloves, finely chopped
30 ml/2 tbsp chopped mixed fresh
   herbs, such as parsley, tarragon,
   chives, dill or coriander

TO COAT

30 ml/2 tbsp paprika
30 ml/2 tbsp finely chopped fresh
   parsley
30 ml/2 tbsp toasted sesame seeds
coarsely ground black pepper mixed
   with poppy seeds

1 Divide the cream cheese equally among four small bowls. Into one mix the Cheddar cheese, mustard and mango chutney if using. Season with cayenne pepper and a little salt. Into the second bowl, mix the Roquefort or Stilton cheese and spring onions or chives and season with a little cayenne.

2 Mix the pesto sauce and pine nuts into the third bowl and season with a little cayenne. Mix the chopped garlic and mixed fresh herbs into the last bowl of cream cheese. Cover and refrigerate all four bowls for about 30 minutes, until the cheese is firm enough to handle. Roll each of the different cheese mixtures into small balls, keeping them separate.

3 Lightly dust the Cheddar flavoured balls with paprika, rolling to cover completely. Roll the pesto balls in chopped parsley and the Roquefort balls in sesame seeds. Roll the garlic-herb cheese balls in coarsely ground black pepper and poppy seeds. Arrange the balls on leaves, a plate or in a lined basket and serve with cocktail sticks.

spring
onions

Cheddar
cheese

sesame seeds

garlic

parsley

cream
cheese

poppy
seeds

black
pepper

dry mustard

pesto sauce

Roquefort cheese

paprika

cayenne
pepper

chopped
pine nuts

mango
chutney

Nutty Cheese Balls

These tasty morsels are perfect for nibbling with drinks.

Makes 32

INGREDIENTS
115 g/4 oz cream cheese
115 g/4 oz Roquefort cheese
115 g/4 oz/1 cup chopped walnuts
chopped fresh parsley, to coat
paprika, to coat
salt and freshly ground black pepper

1 Beat the two cheeses together until smooth using an electric beater.

2 Stir in the chopped walnuts and season with salt and pepper.

3 Shape into small balls (about a rounded teaspoonful each). Chill on a baking sheet until firm.

4 Roll half the balls in the chopped parsley and half in the paprika. Serve on cocktail sticks.

Salami and Olive Cheese Wedges

Use good quality salami for best results.

Makes 24

INGREDIENTS
225 g/8 oz cream cheese
5 ml/1 tsp paprika
2.5 ml/½ tsp English mustard powder
50 g/2 oz/2 tbsp stuffed green olives,
    chopped
225 g/8 oz sliced salami
sliced olives, to garnish

1 Beat the cream cheese with the paprika and mustard and mix well. Stir in the chopped olives.

2 Spread the salami slices with the olive mixture and stack five slices on top of each other. Wrap in clear film and chill until firm. With a sharp knife, cut each stack into four wedges. Garnish with additional sliced olives and serve with a cocktail stick through each wedge, to hold the slices together.

Spiced Mixed Nuts

Spices are a delicious addition to mixed roasted nuts.

Makes 350 g/12 oz/2 cups

INGREDIENTS
115 g/4 oz/⅔ cup brazil nuts
115 g/4 oz/⅔ cup cashew nuts
115 g/4 oz/⅔ cup almonds
2.5 ml/½ tsp mild chilli powder
2.5 ml/½ tsp ground coriander
2.5 ml/½ tsp salt
25 g/1 oz/2 tbsp butter, melted

1 Preheat the oven to 180°C/350°F/ Gas 4. Put all the nuts and spices and the salt on to a baking tray and mix well.

2 Pour over the melted butter and bake for 10–15 minutes, stirring until golden brown.

3 Drain on kitchen paper and allow to cool before serving.

Herby Cheese Biscuits

Use a selection of festive shapes for cutting out these biscuits.

Makes 32

INGREDIENTS
350 g/12 oz/3 cups plain flour
2.5 ml/½ tsp cayenne pepper
5 ml/1 tsp English mustard powder
175 g/6 oz/¾ cup butter
175 g/6 oz strong Cheddar cheese, grated finely
15 ml/1 tbsp mixed dried herbs
1 egg, beaten
salt and freshly ground black pepper

2 Rub the butter into the flour and add the cheese, herbs and seasoning. Stir in the beaten egg to bind, and knead to a smooth dough.

1 Preheat the oven to 200°C/400°F/ Gas 6. Sift the flour, cayenne pepper and mustard powder together into a bowl or food processor.

3 On a lightly floured work surface, roll the dough out thinly. Stamp it into small biscuits with cutters. Bake for 10–15 minutes, or until golden. Cool on a wire rack. Store in an airtight container.

Bombay Prawns

These larger prawns are expensive, so save this dish for a special occasion.

Makes 24

INGREDIENTS

175 ml/6 fl oz/¾ cup olive oil
5 ml/1 tsp ground turmeric (or to taste)
5 ml/1 tsp ground cumin
5 ml/1 tsp garam masala or curry powder
2.5 ml/½ tsp salt
2.5 ml/½ tsp cayenne pepper (or to taste)
juice of 2 limes
24 large uncooked Madagascar or tiger prawns, shelled and deveined, tails attached
coriander leaves, to garnish

limes

shelled prawns

olive oil

turmeric   cumin

garam
masala

coriander

cayenne
pepper

1 In a medium-sized bowl, whisk together well the oil, turmeric, cumin, garam masala, salt, cayenne pepper and lime juice.

2 With a small sharp knife, slit three-quarters of the way through each prawn, cutting down the centre back (be careful not to cut right through). Add the prawns to the marinade and allow to stand in a cool place for 40 minutes.

3 Preheat the grill. Arrange the prawns on a foil-lined grill pan in a single layer. Drizzle over a little of the marinade. Grill for about 2 to 3 minutes, until the prawns are glazed and curled. Serve immediately, on cocktail sticks if you like, garnished with coriander leaves.

COOK'S TIP

Wrap the prawn tails in small pieces of foil to prevent them catching and burning under the grill, then remove halfway through cooking. Make sure the prawns are cooked through and test one by cutting in half.

Thai-fried Vegetables in Wonton Cups

These crispy cups are an ideal way to serve stir-fried vegetables; use your imagination to vary the fillings.

Makes 24

INGREDIENTS

30 ml/2 tbsp vegetable oil, plus extra for greasing
24 small wonton wrappers
120 ml/4 fl oz/½ cup Hoi Sin sauce or plum sauce (optional)
5 ml/1 tsp sesame oil
1 garlic clove, finely chopped
1 cm/½ in piece fresh root ginger, finely chopped
5 cm/2 in piece of lemon grass, crushed
6–8 asparagus spears, cut into 3 cm/1¼ in pieces
8–10 baby sweetcorn, cut in half lengthways
1 small red pepper, seeded and cut into short slivers
15–30 ml/1–2 tbsp sugar
30 ml/2 tbsp soy sauce
juice of 1 lime
5–10 ml/1–2 tsp Chinese-style chilli sauce (or to taste)
1 tsp *huac nam* or Thai or other fish sauce

lemon grass
red pepper
Hoi Sin sauce
wonton wrappers
baby sweetcorn
vegetable oil
asparagus
sesame oil
soy sauce
lime
garlic

3 Add the sugar, soy sauce, lime juice, chilli sauce and fish sauce and toss well to coat. Stir-fry for 30 seconds longer.

4 Spoon an equal amount of vegetable mixture into each of the prepared wonton cups and serve hot.

1 Preheat the oven to 180°C/350°F/ Gas 4. Lightly grease 24 4 cm/1½ in bun tins. Press 1 wonton wrapper into each cup, turning the edges up to form a cup shape. Bake for 8–10 minutes, until crisp and golden. Carefully remove to a wire rack to cool. If you like, brush each cup with a little Hoi Sin or plum sauce (this will help keep the cups crisp if preparing them in advance).

2 In a wok or large frying pan, heat 30 ml/2 tbsp vegetable oil and the sesame oil until very hot. Add the garlic, ginger and lemon grass and stir-fry for 15 seconds until fragrant. Add the asparagus, sweetcorn and red pepper pieces and stir-fry for 2 minutes until tender crisp.

Tequila Sunset

A variation on the popular party drink which can be mixed and chilled in a jug, ready to pour into glasses, and finished off at the last minute with the addition of crème de cassis and honey.

Serves 1

INGREDIENTS
1 measure/22.5 ml/1½ tbsp clear or golden tequila
5 measures/120 ml/4 fl oz lemon juice, chilled
1 measure/22.5 ml/1½ tbsp orange juice, chilled
10–30 ml/1–2 tbsp clear honey
⅔ measure/15 ml/1 tbsp crème de cassis

crème de cassis

lemon juice

tequila

clear honey

orange juice

1 Pour the tequila and then the lemon and orange juices straight into a well-chilled cocktail glass.

2 Using a swizzle stick, mix the ingredients by twisting the stick between the palms of your hands.

3 Drizzle the honey into the centre of the cocktail and it will fall and create a layer at the bottom of the glass.

4 Add the crème de cassis, but do not stir. It will create a glowing layer above the honey at the bottom of the glass.

VARIATION
To make a Tequila Sunrise, mix 2 parts tequila with 6 parts orange juice and 2 parts grenadine and stir gently together.

Brandy Alexander

A warming digestif, made from a blend of crème de cacao, brandy and double cream, that can be served at the end of the meal with coffee.

Serves 1

INGREDIENTS

1 measure/22.5 ml/1½ tbsp
   brandy
1 measure/22.5 ml/1½ tbsp
   crème de cacao
1 measure/22.5 ml/1½ tbsp
   double cream
whole nutmeg, grated,
   to decorate

crème de cacao

nutmeg

double cream

brandy

VARIATION

Warm the brandy and the double cream gently and add to a blender with the crème de cacao. Whizz until frothy. Serve with a cinnamon stick.

1 Half-fill the cocktail shaker with ice and pour in the brandy, crème de cacao and, finally, the cream.

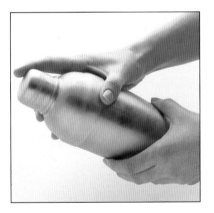

2 Shake for about 20 seconds, to mix together well.

3 Strain the chilled cocktail into a small wine glass.

4 Finely grate a little nutmeg over the top of the cocktail.

Festive Liqueurs

These are easier to make than wines and may be made with a variety of flavours and spirits. All these liqueurs should be allowed to mature for 3 months before drinking.

Makes 850 ml/1½ pints/ 3¾ cups of each liqueur

PLUM BRANDY
450 g/1 lb plums
225 g/8 oz/1 cup demerara sugar
575 ml/1 pint/2½ cups brandy

FRUIT GIN
450 g/1 lb/3 cups raspberries, blackcurrants or sloes
350 g/12 oz/1½ cups granulated sugar
700 ml/1¼ pints/3 cups gin

CITRUS WHISKY
1 large orange
1 small lemon
1 lime
225 g/8 oz/1 cup granulated sugar
575 ml/1 pint/2½ cups whisky

orange

peaches

lemon

lime

blackcurrants

1 Sterilize 3 jars and lids. Wash and halve the plums, remove the stones and finely slice. Place the plums in the sterilized jar with the sugar and brandy. Crack 3 stones, remove the kernels and chop. Add to the jar and stir until well blended.

2 Place the raspberries, blackcurrants or sloes into the prepared jar. If using sloes, prick the surface of the berries using a stainless steel pin to extract the flavour. Add the sugar and gin and stir until well blended.

3 To make the Citrus Whisky, first scrub the fruit. Using a sharp knife or potato peeler pare the rind from the fruit, taking care not to include the white pith. Squeeze out all the juice and place in the jar with the fruit rinds. Add the sugar and whisky, stir until well blended.

4 Cover the jars with lids or double thickness plastic tied well down. Store the jars in a cool place for 3 months.

5 Shake the Fruit Gin every day for 1 month, and then occasionally. Shake the Plum Brandy and Citrus Whisky every day for 2 weeks, then occasionally. Sterilize the chosen bottles and corks or stoppers for each liqueur.

6 When each liqueur is ready to be bottled, strain, then pour into the bottles through a funnel fitted with a filter paper. Fit the corks or stoppers and label with a festive label.

Mulled Red Wine

Excellent to serve on a cold winter's evening; it will really get the party started.

Makes 900 ml/1¹/₂ pints/2¹/₂ cups

INGREDIENTS
1 bottle red wine
75 g/3 oz/6 tbsp soft light brown sugar
2 cinnamon sticks
1 lemon, sliced
4 whole cloves
150 ml/¹/₄ pint/²/₃ cup brandy or port
lemon slices, to serve

2 Strain to remove the spices and lemon slices.

I Put all the ingredients, except the brandy or port, into a large pan. Bring the wine to the boil to dissolve the sugar. Remove, cover the pan and leave it to stand for 5 minutes, to allow the flavours to infuse.

3 Add the brandy and serve warm, with a fresh slice of lemon.

Sparkling Cider Cup

This is a very refreshing, sparkling drink, best served as cold as possible.

Makes 2.6 litres/4¹/₂ pints/10¹/₂ cups

INGREDIENTS
1 orange
1 lemon
1 apple
1 litre/1³/₄ pints/4 cups sparkling
  cider, chilled
1 litre/1³/₄ pints/4 cups lemonade,
  chilled
600 ml/1 pint/2¹/₂ cups apple juice,
  chilled
fresh mint sprigs, to serve

2 Add the cider, lemonade and apple juice. Serve cold with sprigs of fresh mint.

I Slice all the fruit into a large bowl.

Spiced Fruit Cocktail

This non-alcoholic fruit drink is a real treat.

Makes 2 litres/3½ pints/8¾ cups

INGREDIENTS
600 ml/1 pint/2½ cups orange juice,
   chilled
300 ml/½ pint/1¼ cups pineapple
   juice, chilled
pared rind and juice of 1 lemon
4 whole cloves
1 cinnamon stick, broken into pieces
50 g/2 oz/4 tbsp caster sugar
orange slices
ice cubes
600 ml/1 pint/2½ cups sparkling
   mineral water, chilled
600 ml/1 pint/2½ cups ginger ale,
   chilled

1 Mix the orange and pineapple juices together in a large bowl. Add the lemon rind and juice, spices and sugar. Chill.

2 Put the orange slices and ice cubes in a serving bowl. Strain the fruit juice mixture into the bowl. Add the mineral water and ginger ale.

Fruit Punch

This is a quick punch to assemble. Make sure that all the ingredients are well chilled.

Makes 2.5 litres/4¼ pints/10¼ cups

INGREDIENTS
1 bottle white wine, chilled
1 bottle red wine, chilled
45 ml/3 tbsp orange-flavoured liqueur
1 orange, cut in quarters and sliced
seedless grapes
ice cubes
1 litre/1¾ pints/4 cups lemonade

2 Add the orange pieces, grapes and ice, and finally the lemonade.

1 Empty the wines and liqueur into a large bowl.

Gifts & Giving

COUNTRY GIFTS

These practical presents take themes
from nature or use natural products in
the making – perfect ideas for country
visits, hostess gifts or even to keep at
home for decoration.

Needlepoint Cushion

This cushion won't take long to stitch and makes a lovely gift for a fellow needlework enthusiast. The starry theme and trimming of glossy cord give it a Christmassy feel, but its subtle shading will make it a joy to use all year round.

YOU WILL NEED
23 cm (9 in) square of white
   needlepoint canvas with 24 holes
   per 5 cm/12 holes per in
ruler
permanent marker pen
masking tape
small lengths of tapestry wool
   in 12 shades
scissors
tapestry needle
co-ordinating furnishing fabric for
   backing
matching thread
needle
polyester wadding
70 cm (³⁄₄ yd) decorative cord

polyester wadding

backing fabric

needlepoint canvas

tapestry wool

needle

tapestry needle

ruler

scissors

masking tape

permanent marker pen

decorative cord

thread

1 To prepare the canvas, draw a vertical line down the centre and a horizontal line across the centre with a permanent marker pen.

2 Bind the edges of the canvas with masking tape to prevent the yarn from catching as you work. Select three colours for each corner star.

3 Work the design from the chart at the back of the book in tent stitch, beginning in the centre and counting each square as one intersection of canvas threads. Complete all four squares. Remove the masking tape. Press with a steam iron, pulling the canvas gently back into a square. Dry quickly so that the canvas does not distort.

4 Cut a square of backing fabric and pin it to the canvas, right sides together. Machine or hand-stitch around the edges, leaving a gap on one side. Trim the seams and corners and turn to the right side. Stuff with polyester wadding to make a nice plump shape.

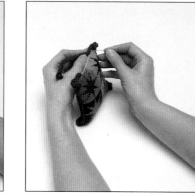

5 Beginning near the opening, hand-stitch the cord around the edges of the cushion. Make a knot in the cord as you reach each corner. Push both ends of the cord into the opening and sew it up neatly, securing the cord as you stitch.

CRAFT TIP

This pincushion is ideal for using up small quantities of tapestry wool left over from other projects, but if you do use scraps make sure you will have enough to complete the design.

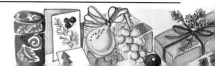

Appliqué Christmas Tree

A charmingly simple little picture which you can frame or mount on card as a seasonal greeting for a special person. Contrasting textures in the homespun fabrics and simple, childlike stitches give it a naïve appeal.

YOU WILL NEED
scraps of homespun fabrics in greens, red and orange
scissors
matching thread
needle
coarse off-white cotton
pins
stranded embroidery thread
gold embroidery thread
iron
picture frame

gold embroidery thread

embroidery thread

thread

scissors

coarse off-white cotton

needle

pins

scraps of homespun fabrics

1 Following the template at the back of the book, cut out the pieces for the Christmas tree from three different shades and textures of green fabric. Cut out a red rectangle for the background and an orange stem. Join the three sections of the tree with running stitches.

2 Pin all the pieces to a backing of off-white cotton, large enough to fill your picture frame.

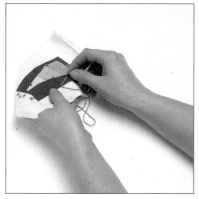

3 Sew the pieces together invisibly in slip-stitch, tucking the edges under with your needle as you sew. Aim for a slightly uneven, naïve appearance. Add gold stars and coloured stitch details using three strands of embroidery thread. Press gently before framing.

Tin Gift Box

Embossed aluminium foil combines festive glitter with the gentle, naïve appeal of tinware, and it's a perfect match for the simplicity of this Shaker box. The embossing is easy to do – simple designs really are the most successful.

YOU WILL NEED
tracing paper
heavy-gauge aluminium foil
masking tape
dried-out ballpoint pen
scissors
gift box
glue-stick

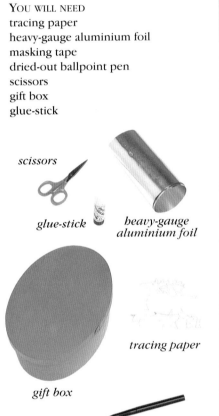

scissors

glue-stick   *heavy-gauge aluminium foil*

tracing paper

gift box

dried-out ballpoint pen

masking tape

1 Trace the reindeer and stars motifs from the back of the book. Attach the tracings to the foil with masking tape and draw over the outlines with an old ballpoint pen.

2 Remove the tracing paper and go over the embossing again if necessary. Cut out the motifs with scissors, leaving a narrow border of about 2 mm (¹/₁₆ in) around the edge – don't cut into the embossing.

3 Add more embossed details to the motifs if you wish.

4 Turn the motifs over and arrange them on the box lid and sides. Attach them using a glue-stick applied liberally.

Fragrant Herb Pillow

This lovely scented sachet looks as if it has been thickly encrusted with gold. It's made using a cutwork technique in which the different fabrics are revealed as if by magic. It's enjoyable to make and a wonderful gift to receive. Choose fabrics of similar weights but different textures and shades of gold, such as taffeta and lamé.

YOU WILL NEED
four 17 cm (6½ in) squares of
    different gold fabrics
pins
matching thread
sewing machine
sharp-pointed scissors
two 25 cm (10 in) squares of gold
    fabric chosen from the selection
    above
gold braid
needle
fragrant herbs or pot-pourri to fill

*fragrant herbs
and pot-pourri*

gold braid

needle

pins

thread

*sharp-pointed
scissors*

*selection of
gold fabrics*

1 Pin the four 17 cm (6½ in) squares of different gold fabric together.

2 Sewing through all four layers, machine-stitch across the middle of the square in both directions, then stitch a simple star motif in each quarter. Don't worry if the four stars don't match each other exactly – you are aiming for a freehand effect.

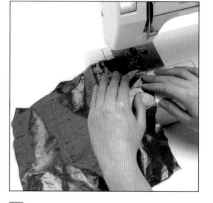

3 With the point of the scissors, pierce the top layer of fabric, then cut out a section of a star. Work around each star, cutting through different areas and layers to reveal the one below, until you are pleased with the effect.

4 Pin the appliqué square in the centre of the right side of one of the large squares and machine-stitch all around the edge. Hand-stitch a length of gold braid over the seam to hide the raw edges.

5 Pin the other gold square to the front of the cushion, right sides together, and machine around the edge with a 1 cm (½ in) seam allowance, leaving an opening down one side.

CRAFT TIP

It is essential to use really sharp, pointed small scissors for this type of appliqué, as you will be cutting through small areas, some of which may be quite delicate and difficult to manoeuvre around.

6 Turn the work right side out, fill loosely with fragrant herbs or pot-pourri and slip-stitch the opening closed.

Yuletide Pot-pourri

Scour ethnic food shops for large bags of bay leaves, cardamom and other exotic ingredients for pot-pourri. Try to include dried flowers (I used hibiscus flowers) for colour and texture.

YOU WILL NEED
oranges
paring knife
large bowl
selection of dried herbs, flowers
    and barks
orris root powder
essential oils
decorative box
cellophane
ribbon

large bowl
cellophane

orris root powder *essential oils*

ribbon

oranges

paring knife

decorative box

dried herbs, flowers and barks

1 Pare the rind from several oranges, keeping the strips as long as possible. Dry them in the lowest shelf of a very low oven and store in a dry place until you are ready to use them. Slices of orange can be dried in the same way and are very decorative in pot-pourri.

2 Mix all the ingredients for the pot-pourri in a large bowl. Do not be tempted to use too many different ingredients or the result will be an untidy-looking mixture.

3 Add the orris root powder, which is used as a fixative for the fragrance, sparingly at first – you do not want to see any residue in the finished mixture. Toss the mixture. Sprinkle with your chosen essential oils.

4 Line a decorative box with a large piece of cellophane and fill generously with the pot-pourri. Gather up the edges and secure with a ribbon.

Fun Wreath

Although every house deserves an elegant fresh Christmas wreath on the front door, all the family can have plenty of fun making this rather alternative wreath. Think of it as a seasonal joke and load it with all the ephemera of Christmas past and present.

YOU WILL NEED
newspaper
adhesive tape
string
scissors
gold spray paint
hot glue gun
assortment of novelties, sweets and
    decorations

scissors

newspaper

*novelties, sweets
and decorations*

*gold spray
paint*

adhesive tape

*hot glue
gun*

string

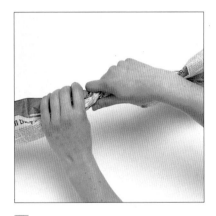

1 Join two sheets of newspaper together down their short sides with adhesive tape. Scrunch up the paper along its length, squeezing it together while gently twisting it to make a paper rope. When it is quite tightly twisted, join the ends with tape to make a ring.

2 Make a second ring in the same way, cutting it a little shorter so that it will fit inside the first ring. Bind the two rings together with string.

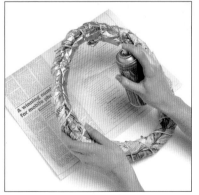

3 Spray the ring on both sides with gold paint and leave to dry.

4 Using a hot glue gun, cover the ring completely with an assortment of Christmas ephemera, such as old decorations, cracker novelties, sweets, decorated pine cones, and bows from gift wrappings.

CHRISTMAS CRAFTS

Nothing is more satisfying than making
Christmas essentials and accessories
yourself – in your own style, and to tone in
with your home decorations and family
traditions. Here are ideas for a toy sack
and stocking, an advent calendar, crackers,
and country-style napkin rings, a table
decoration and a tablecloth for
the main event.

White Christmas Tree

Stand this abstract, modern interpretation of the traditional star-topped Christmas tree on a side table or the mantelpiece. It looks best as part of a cool, monochrome arrangement in white or gold.

YOU WILL NEED
hot glue gun
coarse sisal string
large polystyrene cone
scissors
small polystyrene star
white emulsion paint
paintbrush
gold paint

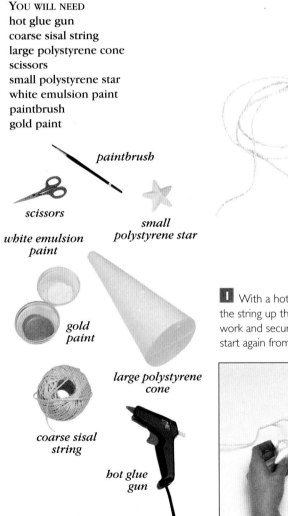

paintbrush

scissors

small polystyrene star

white emulsion paint

gold paint

large polystyrene cone

coarse sisal string

hot glue gun

1 With a hot glue gun, attach the end of the string to the base of the cone. Wind the string up the cone towards the point, then down to the base again, gluing it as you work and securing it where it crosses. Each time you reach the base, cut the string and start again from another point, so that the cone is evenly covered.

2 Wind a short length of string in a coil and glue it to the top of the cone for the star to sit on.

CRAFT TIP

Make sure the ends of the string are evenly spaced around the base of the cone so that it stands upright.

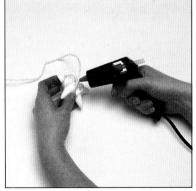

3 Wind and glue string around the star in the same way. Hide the raw ends under the string. Glue the star to the top of the cone.

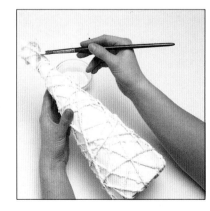

4 Paint the cone and star with several coats of white emulsion paint, covering the string and filling in any unsightly dents in the polystyrene.

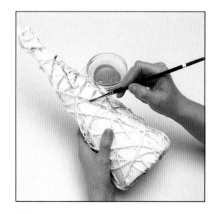

5 Finish by brushing roughly over the string with gold paint.

Gold Crown Tablecloth

Set the festive tone with this lovely white and gold tablecloth. The stencilling is easy and enjoyable to do, but it's important to plan your design carefully before you start work with the paint, so that the motifs are evenly spaced.

YOU WILL NEED
white cotton fabric 135 cm
    (54 in) square
iron
pins
stencil card
craft knife
masking tape
gold stencil paint
stencil brush
fine paintbrush
sewing machine
white thread

stencil card

white thread

masking tape

craft knife

gold stencil paint

fine paintbrush

stencil brush

white cotton fabric

pins

1 Iron the fabric to remove creases, then fold in quarters and press the folds. Fold each quarter to find the centre point, press and mark with pins. Copy the crown and shooting star templates from the back of the book, transfer onto stencil card and cut out with a craft knife. Stencil the crowns in the corners, then the edges and finally the centre.

2 Stencil the shooting stars between the crowns, all pointing in the same direction around the edge of the cloth.

3 Complete the stars by touching up the gaps left by the stencil with a fine brush and gold stencil paint.

4 Press on the wrong side of the fabric to fix the paint. Hem the fabric all around the edge on a sewing machine.

CRAFT TIP
Don't overload your brush, as too much paint may bleed underneath the edges of the stencil.

Sparkling Flowerpot

This shiny flowerpot is covered with the foil wrappings from chocolates and sweets. You'll need to prepare in advance by eating plenty of foil-wrapped chocolates. Choose the colours carefully, and don't forget to save the wrappers! Fill the pot with baubles for a table decoration.

YOU WILL NEED
coloured foil sweet wrappers
terracotta flowerpot
PVA glue
paintbrush

paintbrush

PVA glue

coloured foil sweet wrappers

terracotta flowerpot

1 Smooth out the coloured foil wrappers and select as many rectangular shapes as possible. If any wrappers have tears, you may be able to hide these by overlapping them with perfect pieces.

2 Paint the flowerpot all over with PVA glue to seal the surface.

3 Paint the back of a piece of foil with PVA glue and apply it to the pot, smoothing it with the paintbrush and brushing on more glue to secure it. Continue adding the foil wrappers in an attractive pattern. When the pot is completely covered, seal it inside and out with another coat of glue.

CRAFT TIP

Although you can arrange the foils in a haphazard manner for a crazy patchwork effect, this project looks best if you keep to a more regular design by placing the foil pieces horizontally and vertically.

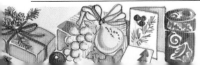

Willow Twig Napkin Rings

You can decorate with natural, homespun materials but still achieve a sparkling effect if you choose bright, glowing colours. Using glue to assemble these rings reinforces the fabric and is a welcome shortcut if making a large quantity.

YOU WILL NEED
willow twigs
secateurs
11 x 22 cm (4½ x 9 in) coarsely
   woven cotton fabric per ring
fabric glue
paintbrush
stranded embroidery thread
needle
scissors
pins
matching thread

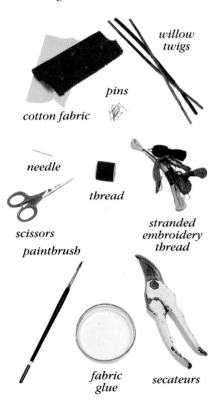

cotton fabric

willow twigs

pins

needle

thread

scissors

paintbrush

stranded embroidery thread

fabric glue

secateurs

1 Cut four pieces of twig, each 9 cm (3½ in) long.

2 Make a 1 cm (½ in) hem along one short end of the fabric and glue it down. Fold the long sides of the fabric rectangle to the centre and glue.

3 Position the twigs evenly across the centre of the right side of the fabric. Using three strands of embroidery thread oversew the twigs on to the napkin ring.

4 Pin the ends of the ring together, tucking the raw edge into the folded edge. Slip-stitch together.

Holly Leaf Napkin

The Christmas table deserves something more distinctive than paper napkins, and your guests will love these specially embroidered cotton ones in festive but definitely non-traditional colours. The holly leaf motif is quick and easy to work in stem stitch.

YOU WILL NEED
paper for template
scissors
50 cm (20 in) square of washable cotton fabric in hot pink for each napkin
pins
tailor's chalk
stranded embroidery thread in acid green, acid yellow and bright orange
needle

cotton fabric   *paper*

          pins

tailor's chalk

stranded embroidery thread

scissors

needle

1 Trace the holly leaf motif from the back of the book and use it to make a paper template. Pin it to one corner of the fabric, allowing room for a hem, and draw round it with tailor's chalk.

2 Using three strands of embroidery thread and working in stem stitch, embroider the outline of the holly leaf in acid green and the veins in acid yellow.

3 Fold under and pin a 5 mm (¼ in) double hem all around the napkin.

4 Using three strands of bright orange embroidery thread, work a neat running stitch evenly around the hem.

Christmas Crackers

Making your own Christmas crackers is really rewarding and it's great fun watching friends and family pull them open to discover the treats inside. Make exactly the number you need for your party and collect small gifts to put in them.

YOU WILL NEED
double-sided crêpe paper in
    bright colours
craft knife
metal ruler
cutting mat
thin card in black and white
double-sided adhesive tape
cracker snaps
paper hats, jokes and gifts to
    go in the crackers
narrow black ribbon
gold paper-backed foil
corrugated cardboard
gold crêpe paper
fine gold cord

metal ruler

craft knife

cracker snaps

gold crêpe paper

double-sided crêpe paper

fine gold cord

narrow black ribbon

thin card

gold paper-backed foil

paper hats, jokes and gifts

double-sided adhesive tape

1 For each cracker, cut two rectangles of crêpe paper measuring 25 x 20 cm (10 x 8 in). Join them together, overlapping the ends, to make a rectangle 45 x 20 cm (18 x 8 in).

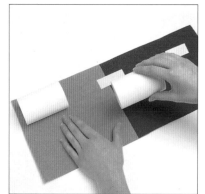

2 Cut three pieces of thin white card 22 x 10 cm (9 x 4 in). Roll each into a cylinder, overlapping the short ends by 3.5 cm (1¼ in). Lay strips of double-sided adhesive tape across the crêpe paper with which to attach the card cylinders: one in the centre and the other two about 4 cm (1½ in) in from each end of the rectangle. Roll up and secure the edge with double-sided tape.

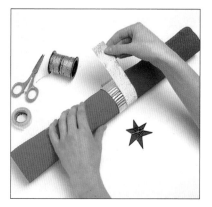

3 Decorate the cracker with strips of the gold papers. To make the corrugated paper, lay a strip of paper-backed foil over a piece of corrugated cardboard and ease the foil into the ridges with your thumb. Cut a simple star shape from thin black card, wrap some fine gold cord around it and stick it on top of the gold decorations (use one of the star templates at the back of the book or draw your own).

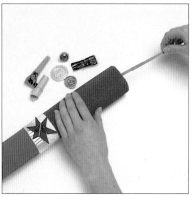

4 Insert the snap and place the novelties and a paper hat in the central section of the cracker.

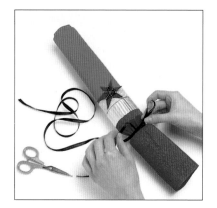

5 Tie up the ends with narrow black ribbon, easing the crêpe paper gently, so that you can tie the knots very tightly.

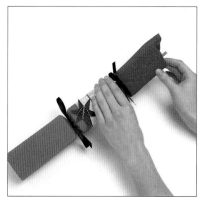

6 Complete the cracker by folding the edges of the crêpe paper over the ends of the card cylinders.

Santa's Toy Sack

Leave this gorgeous sack by the fireplace on Christmas Eve and Santa's guaranteed to fill it. Alternatively, it would be a wonderful way to deliver all your gifts if you're visiting friends. The contrast in texture between the luxurious satin ribbons and the coarse weave of the sack is novel and effective.

YOU WILL NEED

1.6 x 1.1 m (1 ¾ x 1¾ yd) hessian, washed
tape measure
scissors
pins
sewing machine
selection of contrasting satin ribbons, 3.5 – 4.5 cm (1¼–1¾ in) wide
matching thread
needle

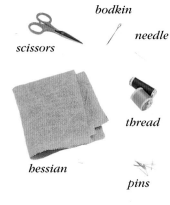

bodkin

needle

scissors

thread

hessian

pins

tape measure

satin ribbons

1 Trim the washed hessian so that it measures 1 x 1.5 m (39 x 55 in). Fold it in half, right sides together, bringing the shorter sides together, and pin across the bottom and up the side, making a seam allowance of approximately 4 cm (1½ in).

2 Machine-stitch the bottom and one side of the sack.

4 With a bodkin, or safety pin, thread a length of contrasting ribbon through the channel you have created. Make sure it is long enough to make a generous bow when the top of the sack is gathered up. Turn the sack the right side out.

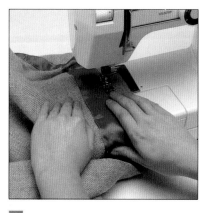

3 Still working on the wrong side, turn down the top edge by approximately 7 cm (3 in). Pin, then cover the raw edge with a length of satin ribbon. Fold under the raw ends of the ribbon to leave an opening. Machine-stitch close to the top and bottom edges of the ribbon.

5 Using a double thread, stitch along one edge of a length of ribbon in running stitch. Draw the ribbon up into tight gathers and measure how much you need to make a rosette, allowing for joining the ends. You can then cut all the ribbons to this length. Gather again and secure tightly, joining the raw edges invisibly from the wrong side.

6 Make enough rosettes in assorted colours to make a pleasing arrangement on the front of the sack. Stitch on the rosettes by hand.

CRAFT TIP
Hessian is not pre-shrunk, so wash the fabric before you begin to make the sack. Use your machine's hottest setting, then press with a steam iron or damp cloth to remove all the creases.

Velvet Stocking

This rather grown-up stocking is so grand that it's just asking to be filled with exquisite treats and presents. Make it in rich, dark colours for a really Christmassy look.

YOU WILL NEED
paper for templates
dress-weight velvet in three
    toning colours
scissors
pins
tailor's chalk
sewing machine
matching thread
decorative braid
sequin ribbon
gold satin fabric
sewing needle
gold buttons

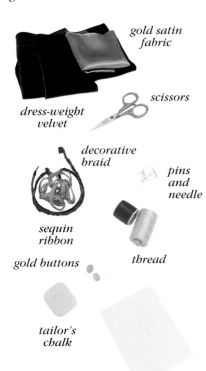

gold satin fabric

scissors

dress-weight velvet

decorative braid

pins and needle

sequin ribbon

gold buttons

thread

tailor's chalk

paper

1 Copy the templates from the back of the book on to paper and increase to the size required. Place the template for each section on a double thickness of each colour velvet. Pin and draw around each pattern piece with tailor's chalk. Cut out, leaving a narrow seam allowance.

2 Pin together the three sections of each side of the stocking and then machine-stitch.

3 On the right side of each piece, pin a strip of decorative braid and a row of sequins. Sew these on invisibly by hand.

4 With right sides together, machine the two sides of the stocking together. Turn through to the right side.

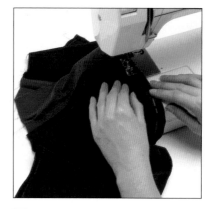

5 Cut out the satin stocking top and machine-stitch the ends together to form a tube. Pin to the top of the stocking, right sides together. Machine-stitch and turn through, leaving a cuff of satin folded over the top of the stocking. Turn in the raw edge on the inside and catch it to the seams of the velvet stocking.

6 Trim the satin cuff with a few gold buttons and attach a loop of decorative braid for hanging.

Christmas Countdown

Christmas is coming! Excitement builds as the windows of an Advent calendar are opened day by day. Paint the façade of this three-dimensional house in hot, bright colours with lots of gilding.

YOU WILL NEED
tracing paper
pencil
thin white card
craft knife
metal ruler
cutting mat
gouache paints
paintbrush
white cartridge paper
watercolour inks
gold marker pen
glue-stick
white polystyrene-filled
   mounting board
multi-cup sequins

mounting board

watercolour ink

gouache paint

glue-stick

craft knife

metal ruler

multi-cup sequins

pencil

gold marker pen

white cartridge paper

tracing paper

paintbrush

1 Enlarge and trace the template for the front of the Advent calendar and transfer it on to a sheet of white card. Cut around three sides of each window with a craft knife.

2 Turn over the sheet and paint the backs of the windows and a little of the area around them with gouache paint, so that they will look neat when the windows are opened.

3 Using the front tracing again, mark the window frames on cartridge paper and draw on the inside motifs. Paint with watercolour inks and draw in details with a gold marker pen. Cut out and attach with a glue-stick.

4 Cut the work into three sections, as shown on the template. Cut three pieces of mounting board, making the largest the size and shape of the whole calendar with two more graded steps to go in front. Mount the pieces of card on the boards, gluing the edges, and glue the sections together.

5 Paint the front of the calendar, carefully avoiding getting any paint inside the windows. Add details and number the windows with a gold marker pen. Don't forget to paint the edges of the mounting boards.

6 Finish the calendar with shiny multi-cup sequins. Using a glue-stick, attach them all around the edges of the Advent calendar.

GIFT-WRAPPING

Everybody likes receiving gifts, and when
they have been wrapped and dressed with
loving care and attention it adds even more
pleasure and satisfaction to the occasion.

Classy Golden Gift Wrap

For a special present, or just to make yours the gift everyone notices under the tree, nothing beats a beautiful golden package. When you are wrapping with gold, make it bold! There are different kinds of gold paper; the brightest is cellophane with a metallic coating on both sides. Matt antique gold paper has a dull gold sheen and is more muted in appearance.

YOU WILL NEED
sheet of gold wrapping paper, depending on size of gift
scissors
double-sided adhesive tape
broad gold ribbon
florist's wire
plastic pear and grapes
antique gold spray paint

spray paint

gold wrapping paper

ribbon

plastic pear and grapes

scissors

florist's wire

double-sided adhesive tape

1 If your gift is not already boxed, find a box of a suitable size. Using the side of the box as a measuring guide, trim the paper to fit. You need no more than a 7.5 cm (3 in) overlap, and the ends should fold into neat triangles, with no bulky seams.

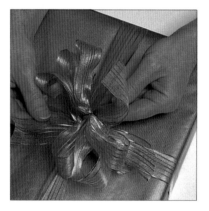

4 Make a large bow, securing the loops of ribbon in the centre with a binding of florist's wire, then cover the wire with a double thickness of ribbon, tying it loosely and tucking the ends under the bow, and using them to tie it to the box ribbons.

3 Cut a long length of ribbon and tie it around the box, crossing over underneath and tying firmly on the top. Trim off the ends.

CRAFT TIP

Try to find gold ribbon in a slightly deeper shade than the paper and choose trimmings that co-ordinate well. You can either spray the plastic fruit with antique gold aerosol, or use gilt cream, that is simply rubbed on to the surface and buffed when dry.

2 Use double-sided adhesive tape inside the top seam and at the centre points of the ends, to secure the paper invisibly.

5 Apply the gold spray to the fruit and, when dry, make up a bunch of the grapes and the pear.

6 Attach the fruit to the top of the box by twisting florist's wire around the ribbon.

Rubber Bands and Sealing Wax

Children love doing up parcels but their enthusiasm for the roll of adhesive tape may leave you feeling exasperated! Rubber bands are the perfect alternative to tape!

Sealing wax recalls the days when all parcel post had to have string and labels, and be sealed with irregular shapes of hard red wax.

FOR RUBBER BANDS
YOU WILL NEED
parcel-wrap
scissors
pack of coloured rubber bands
small folded card

FOR SEALING WAX
YOU WILL NEED
checked paper
scissors
double-sided adhesive tape
coarse, thick string
sealing wax stick
cigarette lighter
gift tag

paper   *parcel-wrap*

gift tag

sealing wax   *folded card*

string

cigarette lighter   *rubber bands*

scissors

1 For the rubber bands, wrap the parcel, then stretch the bands lengthways and crossways to secure the flaps.

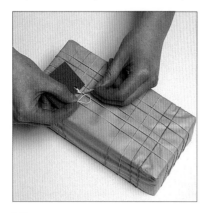

2 Add a criss-cross pattern in a sequence of colours. Loop a rubber band through the holes punched in the card, and tie it on to the gift.

3 For the sealing wax, wrap the gift with tape. Wind a long length of the string around the parcel three times. Loop the string around the three strands, knot it, then take it along the top of the parcel. Hold it in place, wrap the remaining string round three times, bringing the end up to loop around the crosspiece. Tie a knot.

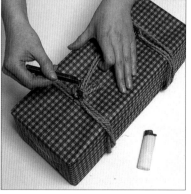

4 Light the sealing wax wick and let the hot wax drip on to all the knots, then dip all the loose string ends in sealing wax. The hardened wax will hold the knots in place. Attach a gift tag to the string if you wish.

Bold Red and Gold

There is something sumptuous about red tissue paper – the rustling noise and smooth texture seem to impart a sense of luxury, and the colour deepens with layering. Stamp the paper with large gold stars and you will have one of the most stunning gift-wraps around.

YOU WILL NEED
pack of red tissue paper
big star rubber stamp
gold ink
saucer
adhesive tape
scissors
gold ribbon, cord or tinsel

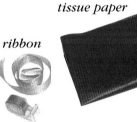

tissue paper

ribbon

adhesive tape   *gold ink*

scissors   *rubber stamp*

1 Lay a sheet of tissue paper on to scrap paper and, beginning in one corner, work diagonally across the sheet, stamping stars about 5 cm (2 in) apart. Leave to dry.

2 Wrap the gift using a lining of one or two sheets of plain red tissue paper under the stamped sheet. Use adhesive tape to secure the ends. (If desired, you could use double-sided adhesive tape for invisible joins.)

3 Trim the gift with a gold ribbon tied on top with a single bow.

4 Swallowtail the ribbon ends for a professional finish.

Season's Greetings – the Natural Look

This project will appeal to those who feel a sense of visual indigestion when faced with all the glitz of Christmas.

A sheet of plain brown parcel-wrap is folded around the gift, then a light, airy collage of festive tissue paper shapes is applied. The gift is tied up with coarse brown string and decorated with cones and pods.

YOU WILL NEED
parcel-wrap
scissors
double-sided adhesive tape
pencil
tracing paper
white chalk
dark blue and orange tissue
  paper
PVA glue
thick, coarse string
selection of dried cones and
  pods
hot glue gun

tracing paper

hot glue gun

cones and pods

PVA glue

scissors

coarse string

double-sided adhesive tape

parcel-wrap

tissue paper

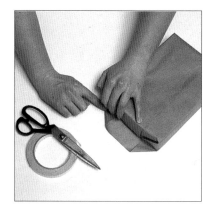

1 Use the box as a measuring guide and cut the parcel-wrap to size.

2 Wrap the box using double-sided adhesive tape.

3 Trace the shapes from the back of the book and cut them out of blue and orange tissue paper. Use chalk to transfer the shapes on to the darker paper. The number you will need depends upon the size of your gift.

4 Experiment with the positioning of the shapes until you are happy with the arrangement, then apply a thin layer of glue, spread with your finger, directly on to the paper. Quickly smooth the tissue shapes on to the glue.

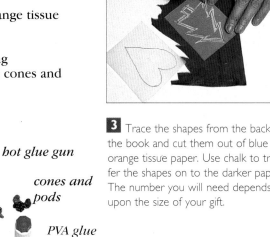

5 Tie coarse string around the gift, crossing it over underneath and knotting it on top. Untwist the string ends and fluff them out, then trim neatly.

6 Use the glue gun to stick a small arrangement of miniature cones and pods to the knotted string.

The Ice Box

A great big box under the Christmas tree always attracts attention, but this stunning present is in danger of upstaging the Christmas tree itself!

   The blue paper is stencilled with snowflakes, then the whole gift is bunched up in clear icy cellophane. Foil ribbons and Christmas tree ornaments complete the effect.

YOU WILL NEED
tracing paper
pencil
cardboard or mylar
craft knife
bright blue paper
small sponge
bowl of water
white watercolour paint
saucer
adhesive tape
scissors
roll of clear, wide cellophane
silver foil ribbon
selection of Christmas tree
   ornaments

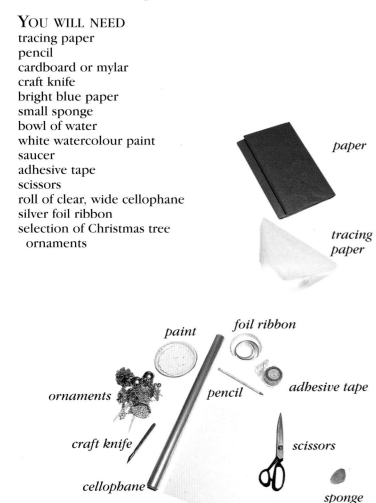

paper

tracing paper

paint *foil ribbon*

ornaments *pencil* *adhesive tape*

craft knife *scissors*

cellophane *sponge*

mylar

1 Trace and cut out the stencil at the back of the book. You can use cereal box cardboard or special stencil plastic called mylar. Take care when using the craft knife.

2 Place scrap paper on your work surface and use a small sponge to apply the white paint. Dip the sponge in the bowl of water then squeeze it out thoroughly. Stencil paints should always be on the dry side to prevent any from seeping under the stencil. Apply the snowflakes randomly all over the blue paper and right over the edges. Allow to dry thoroughly.

3 If one sheet of paper is not big enough to cover the box, lay two sheets side by side and run a length of adhesive tape along the join. Repeat with other sheets until you have a single sheet large enough for the box. Wrap up the box, using adhesive tape to hold the wrapping securely in place.

4 Unroll a length of cellophane on your work surface long enough to pass under the box, up the sides and allowing at least 30 cm (12 in) extra on both ends. Do the same in the other direction, to cross over the first sheet under the box.

CRAFT TIP

This gift-wrap really works best on a large scale, so if you have a boxed toy, stereo or television to wrap, look no further.

5 Gather up the cellophane on top of the box, making sure that the sides of the box are completely covered, then tape around the bunch, close to the box top.

6 Cover the adhesive tape with silver foil ribbon and attach the Christmas tree decorations.

Collage Gift-wrap

Look along the racks on the newspaper stand for interesting foreign scripts to incorporate in this fascinating gift-wrap. The newspaper is painted with translucent watercolour inks so that the print shows through.

YOU WILL NEED
foreign language newspaper
watercolour inks
paintbrush
white cartridge paper
coloured card
stencil card
craft knife
gold and black stencil paint
kitchen sponge
scissors
corrugated card
plain gold gift-wrap
glue-stick

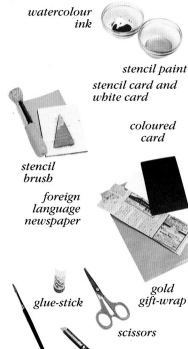

watercolour ink

stencil paint

stencil card and white card

coloured card

stencil brush

foreign language newspaper

glue-stick

gold gift-wrap

scissors

craft knife

paintbrush

1 Paint sections of the newspaper in bright watercolour inks.

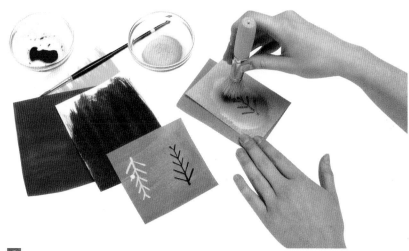

2 Transfer the Christmas tree template at the back of the book to a piece of stencil card and cut out. Paint plain white cartridge paper in different coloured inks or use coloured card. Stencil the paper in black and gold.

3 Cut a triangular Christmas tree shape out of kitchen sponge and stick it to a piece of corrugated card. Stamp some of the coloured newsprint with gold trees.

4 Tear strips, rectangles and simple tree shapes from the coloured newsprint. Tear around the stamped and stencilled motifs, and cut some out with scissors to give a different texture.

5 Arrange the motifs on the gold gift-wrap and attach them down using a glue-stick.

Wrapping Unusual Shapes

Not all gifts come in convenient shapes and sizes for wrapping. While a stock of tubes and boxes may help wrap an awkwardly shaped gift, you may not always have a suitable container to hand.

Trimmings

The finishing touches to your present are all-important. The simple tying of an attractive bow can transform a gift. Here are just a few suggestions for completing your gift-wrap.

TYING A BASIC BOW

1 Decide on a surface that is going to be the base; in this case the teddy is able to sit up. Cut out a regular shape, either square, rectangular or round, from thick cardboard. Cover with a piece of your gift-wrap.

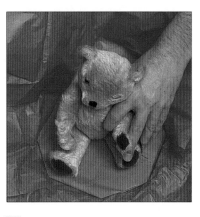

2 Place the cardboard in the middle of a large sheet of paper, or cross two lengths over for a larger gift.

3 Pull up the paper from opposite sides and bunch it up on top of the gift. Tissue paper works well for this, because it creases in an attractive way. If you are using thicker paper, gather and pleat it as you make the bunch.

4 Tie a ribbon or cord firmly around the bunch, then arrange the paper into a balanced decorative shape. An ornament hanging down from the ribbon will help to draw attention back down to the gift.

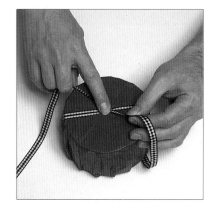

1 Pass the ribbon under the gift so that you have two ends of equal length. Tie the two together at the top.

2 Knot the tied ends so that both your hands are freed for tying the bow.

3 Form two loops and tie together to make a simple bow.

4 Finish off the bow by cutting the ribbon ends into swallowtails. Fold the ribbon down the middle then cut from the fold towards the open edges at a slant. Make the cut towards the ends of the ribbon.

Different Ways of Fastening Gifts

STRING AND RIBBON

1 Wrap your gift in tissue paper, then wind coarse string around the box at least four times in each direction.

2 Take a short, narrow red ribbon and use it to gather all the string together at the centre point. Tie a simple bow in the red ribbon and separate the strands of string out towards the edges of the box.

PINK AND GREY GIFT

1 Use a broad, fancy ribbon on a plain background. Cross the ribbon over on top of the box, then take the ends around underneath it.

2 Instead of tying the ribbon in a bow or knot, use double-sided adhesive tape to join it and give a taut, flat finish. The ribbon is shown off without the need for additional decoration.

PURPLE AND GOLD GIFT

1 Wrap a gift box in several layers of deep purple tissue paper, then surround it with a rope of gold.

2 Tie a double knot and let the tasselled ends fall across the gift as a decoration. Experiment with scarves, tie-backs and even pyjama cords!

PINK ON PINK GIFT

1 Wrap the gift in pink tissue paper and tie it up with a pink spotted ribbon.

2 Thread a biscuit cutter (this one is in the shape of a Christmas tree) on to the ribbon and tie a small bow. Christmas biscuit cutters make great decorative tags, and with luck you may even get some biscuits baked for you!

CARDS & TAGS

Here are lively ideas for making cards and
labels to complete your parcels – from
edible tags to shaker-style patterns and
cards made in natural and recycled
materials.

Recycled Look

There is a huge variety of rough-textured, hand-made papers and card around, many imported from the East and made from unusual exotic plants. Some have visible fibres, flowers or leaves and others are finer, with embossed textures applied to them.

YOU WILL NEED
black corrugated card
scissors
eyelets and punch
3 contrasting sheets of hand-
  made textured paper
PVA glue
raffia
selection of tissue paper scraps
hole punch
coarse string

card and paper

hole punch

scissors

eyelets and punch

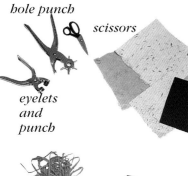

raffia

PVA glue

string

1 For a star tag, draw a star and cut the shape from tissue paper. Cut a disc from handmade paper, spread it lightly with PVA glue and press the star on to it.

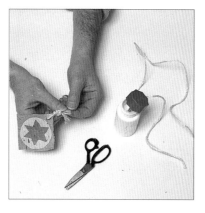

2 Cut a square to give a 1 cm (½ in) border to the disc, from contrasting handmade paper. Punch a hole in one corner and thread it with coarse string. Tie a knot and untwist the end to make a tassel.

3 To make a heart and bow, cut a rectangle from the black corrugated card and fix an eyelet in the centre at one end.

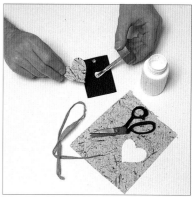

4 Cut a heart from textured paper, and glue it, point down, at the other end of the rectangle. Thread some raffia through the eyelet and tie a bow that rests above the heart.

Pierced Patterns

These folk-art-influenced labels have patterns pricked through, like the old tinware used in lamps and kitchen cupboards. A simple motif can be depicted on a piece of metallic or plain card by pricking out holes at regular distances apart, then the shape can be made ornate by the addition of holes of different sizes.

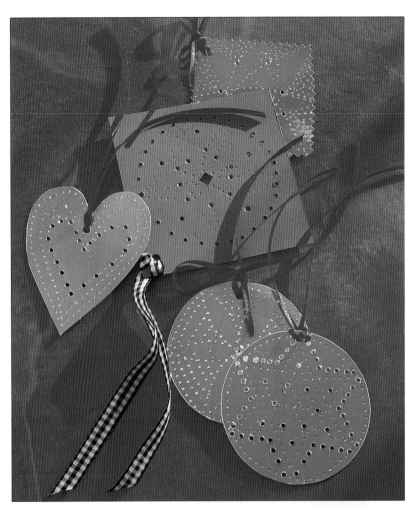

YOU WILL NEED
scissors
metallic card
pair of compasses
dressmaker's pattern wheel,
   or selection of pins, needles
   and nails
hole punch
ribbon

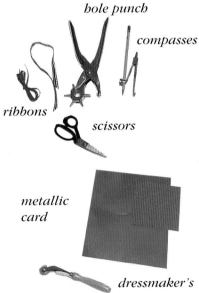

hole punch

compasses

ribbons

scissors

metallic card

dressmaker's pattern wheel

1 Cut out several different shapes from the metallic card. Use a pair of compasses to draw the pinwheel pattern on the back of the card.

CRAFT TIP
A multi-sized hole punch is useful, but a series of nails in different sizes and pins will also produce interesting results.

2 Practise to get the feel of the pattern wheel, then, pressing evenly and firmly, use it to go over the pattern. Draw the other patterns in the same way.

3 Add a few strategically placed larger holes with the punch or a nail, then make a hole and thread with ribbon to complete the gift tag.

Edible Labels

These spice-biscuit labels have the great advantage of wafting delicious smells around the house while they bake. A word of warning – tie them to the gifts at the last moment, lest the temptation to nibble is too great and the result is a pile of unnamed presents!

YOU WILL NEED
ready-mixed biscuit dough
rolling pin
board
biscuit cutters
ready-mixed icing
ribbon

biscuit cutters

ready-mixed icing

ribbon

*biscuit dough mixture
rolling pin
board*

1 Roll out the dough to 1 cm (½ in) thick and cut out the biscuits using different-shaped cutters. Make holes for the ribbon (using a skewer is easiest). Bake in the oven at 180°C/350°F/Gas 4 for 10–12 minutes. Transfer to a wire rack to cool.

2 Decorate the biscuits by piping on ready-mixed icing.

3 Thread the biscuit labels with thin ribbon.

4 Tie red ribbon around the gift and secure the edible label, so that it lies flat on top of the parcel.

COOK'S TIP
Remember to make a hole in your biscuit labels before you bake them.

Elegant Embossed Cards

Embossed paper has a very subtle, expensive look about it, but is in fact not at all difficult to make. There are several different methods, but for a unique card or label the simplest way to do it is to place the paper over a stencil on a flat surface, and simply rub the back of the paper.

YOU WILL NEED
ready-cut stencil or card
  cut-out
coloured paper, card and
  envelopes
embossing tool – blunt,
  smooth-ended plastic
scissors
PVA glue

PVA glue

scissors   *coloured paper*

paper

envelopes

embossing tool

stencil

1 Place the heart stencil from the back of the book on a flat work surface and cover it with the paper.

2 Holding down firmly, begin rubbing the paper gently over the cut-out area to define the shape. Increase the pressure until the shape shows up as a clear indentation. Turn the paper over to reveal the embossed shape.

3 Trim the paper to shape and stick it on to a red card background. Pair it up with a contrasting envelope or punch a hole in it, thread with ribbon and use it as a gift tag, if you wish.

CRAFT TIP
You can cut a shape for embossing from thin card. Experiment with different papers too; they all give different results. Remember that if it is too thin it will tear easily, so thicker paper is best.

EDIBLE GIFTS

Home-made edible gifts are a true
expression of the country festival spirit,
and the perfect way to spread an
atmosphere of goodwill amongst friends
and guests throughout the holidays.

Marzipan Fruits

These eye-catching and realistic fruits will make a perfect gift for lovers of marzipan.

Makes 450 g/1 lb

INGREDIENTS
450 g/1 lb white marzipan
yellow, green, red, orange and
    burgundy food colouring dusts
30 g/2 tbsp whole cloves

marzipan

cloves

food colouring dusts

1 Cover a baking sheet with non-stick baking paper. Cut the marzipan into quarters. Take 1 piece and cut it into 10 even-sized pieces. Place a little of each of the food colouring dusts into a palette, or place small amounts spaced apart on a plate. Cut ⅔ of the cloves into 2 pieces, making a stem and core end.

2 Taking the 10 pieces, shape each one into a neat ball. Dip 1 ball into the yellow food colouring dust and roll between the palms of the hands to colour. Re-dip into the green colouring and re-roll to tint a greeny-yellow colour. Using your forefinger, roll one end of the ball to make a pear shape. Press a clove stem into the top and a core end into the base. Repeat with the remaining 9 balls of marzipan. Place on the baking sheet.

3 Cut another piece of the marzipan into 10 pieces and shape into balls. Dip each piece into green food colouring dust and roll in the palms to colour evenly. Add a spot of red colouring dust and roll to blend the colour. Using a ball tool or the end of a paintbrush, indent the top and base to make an apple shape. Insert a stem and core.

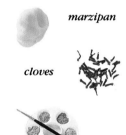

4 Repeat as above using another piece of the marzipan to make 10 orange coloured balls. Roll each over the surface of a fine grater to give the texture of an orange skin. Press a clove core into the base of each.

5 Take the remaining piece of marzipan, reserve a small piece, and mould the rest into lots of tiny marzipan beads. Colour them burgundy with the food colouring dust. Place a whole clove on the baking sheet. Arrange a cluster of burgundy beads in the shape of a bunch of grapes. Repeat with the remaining burgundy beads of marzipan to make another 3 bunches of grapes.

6 Roll out the remaining tiny piece of marzipan thinly and brush with green food colouring dust. Using a small vine leaf cutter, cut out 8 leaves, mark the veins with a knife and place 2 on each bunch of grapes, bending to give a realistic appearance. When all the marzipan fruits are dry, pack into gift boxes.

Turkish Delight

Turkish Delight is always a favourite at Christmas, and this versatile recipe can be made in minutes. Try different flavours such as lemon, crème de menthe and orange and vary the colours accordingly.

Makes 450 g/1 lb

INGREDIENTS

450 g/1 lb/2 cups granulated sugar
300 ml/½ pint/1¼ cups water
25 g/1 oz powdered gelatine
½ tsp tartaric acid
30 ml/2 tbsp rose-water
pink food colouring
25 g/1 oz/3 tbsp icing sugar, sifted
15 g/1 tbsp cornflour

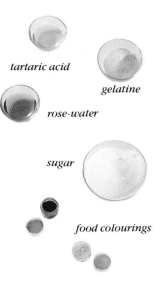

tartaric acid

gelatine

rose-water

sugar

food colourings

1 Wet the insides of 2 × 18 cm/7 in shallow square tins with water. Place the sugar and all but 60 ml/4 tbsp of water into a heavy-based saucepan. Heat gently, stirring occasionally, until the sugar has dissolved.

2 Blend the gelatine and remaining water in a small bowl and place over a saucepan of hot water. Stir occasionally until dissolved. Bring the sugar syrup to the boil and boil steadily for about 8 minutes or until the syrup registers 127°C/260°F on a sugar thermometer. Stir the tartaric acid into the gelatine, then pour into the boiling syrup and stir until well blended. Remove from the heat.

3 Add the rose-water and a few drops of pink food colouring to tint the mixture pale pink. Pour the mixture into the tins and allow to set for several hours or overnight. Dust a sheet of greaseproof paper with some of the icing sugar and cornflour. Dip the base of the tin in hot water. Invert onto the paper. Cut into 2.5 cm/1 in squares using an oiled knife. Toss in icing sugar to coat evenly.

Truffle Christmas Puddings

Truffles disguised as Christmas puddings are great fun to make and receive. Make any flavoured truffle, and decorate them as you like.

Makes 20

INGREDIENTS
20 plain chocolate truffles
15 g/1 tbsp cocoa
15 g/1 tbsp icing sugar
225 g/8 oz/1 cup white chocolate
    dots, melted
50 g/2 oz white marzipan
green and red food colourings
yellow food colouring dust

marzipan

chocolate truffles

food colouring dust

white chocolate dots

1 Sift the cocoa and icing sugar together and coat the truffles.

2 Spread ⅔ of the melted white chocolate over a piece of non-stick baking paper. Pick up the corners and shake to level the surface. Using a 2.5 cm/1 in daisy cutter, stamp out 20 rounds when the chocolate has just set. Place a truffle on the centre of each daisy shape, secured with a little of the reserved melted chocolate. Leave to set.

3 Colour ⅔ of the marzipan green and ⅓ red using the food colourings. Roll out the green thinly and stamp out 40 leaves using a tiny holly leaf cutter. Mark the veins with a knife. Mould lots of tiny red beads. Colour the remaining white chocolate with yellow food colouring dust and place in a greaseproof paper piping bag. Fold down the top, cut off the point and pipe over the top of each truffle to resemble custard. Arrange the holly leaves and berries on the top. When set, arrange in gift boxes and tie with ribbon.

Glacé Fruits

These luxury sweetmeats are very popular at
Christmas and they cost a fraction of the shop price
if made at home. The whole process takes about 4
weeks, but the result is well worth the effort. Choose
one type of fruit, or select a variety of fruits such as
cherries, plums, peaches, apricots, starfruit, pineapple,
apples, oranges, lemons, limes and clementines.

Makes 24 pieces

INGREDIENTS
450 g/1 lb fruit
1 kg/2¼ lb/4½ cups granulated sugar
115 g/4 oz/1 cup powdered glucose

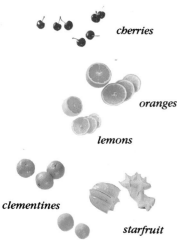

cherries

oranges

lemons

clementines

starfruit

apricots

1 Remove the stones from cherries, plums, peaches and apricots. Peel and core pineapple and cut into cubes or rings. Peel, core and quarter apples and thinly slice citrus fruits. Prick the skins of cherries with a stainless steel needle so the syrup can penetrate the skin.

2 Place enough of the prepared fruit in a saucepan to cover the base, keeping individual fruit types together. Add enough water to cover the fruit and simmer very gently, to avoid breaking it, until almost tender. Use a slotted spoon to lift the fruit and place in a shallow dish, removing any skins if necessary. Repeat as above until all the fruit has been cooked.

3 Measure 300 ml/½ pint/1¼ cups of the liquid, or make up this quantity with water if necessary. Pour into the saucepan and add 50 g/2 oz/4 tbsp sugar and the glucose. Heat gently, stirring occasionally, until dissolved. Bring to the boil and pour over the fruit in the dish, completely immersing it, and leave overnight.

4 DAY 2. Drain the syrup from the fruit into the saucepan and add 50 g/2 oz/4 tbsp sugar. Heat gently to dissolve the syrup and bring to the boil. Pour over the fruit and leave overnight. Repeat this process each day, draining off the syrup, dissolving 50 g/2 oz/4 tbsp sugar, boiling the syrup and immersing the fruit and leaving overnight on Days 3, 4, 5, 6 and 7.

5 DAY 8. Drain the fruit, dissolve 75 g/3 oz/½ cup sugar in the syrup and bring to the boil. Add the fruit and cook gently for 3 minutes. Return to the dish and leave for 2 days. DAY 10. Repeat as above for Day 8; at this stage the syrup should look like clear honey. Leave in the dish for at least a further 10 days, or up to 3 weeks.

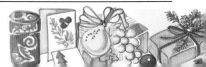

6 Place a wire rack over a tray and remove each piece of fruit with a slotted spoon. Arrange on the rack. Dry the fruit in a warm dry place or in the oven at the lowest setting until the surface no longer feels sticky. To coat in sugar, spear each piece of fruit and plunge into boiling water, then roll in granulated sugar. To dip into syrup, place the remaining sugar and 175 ml/6 fl oz/¾ cup of water in a saucepan. Heat gently until the sugar has dissolved, then boil for 1 minute. Dip each piece of fruit into boiling water, then quickly into the syrup. Place on the wire rack and leave in a warm place until dry. Place the fruits in paper sweet cases and pack into boxes.

Smokie Spread

This wonderful spread will be a welcome change of flavour at Christmas. Spread it on hot toast for an instant snack.

Makes enough to fill 4 small ramekin dishes

INGREDIENTS
115 g/4 oz/½ cup unsalted butter
350 g/12 oz smokie or kipper fillets, cooked
grated rind and juice of 1 lime
10 ml/2 tsp tomato purée
30 ml/2 tbsp whisky
50 g/2 oz/1 cup wholemeal breadcrumbs
½ tsp freshly ground black pepper

TO GARNISH
4 bay leaves
4 black olives, halved

black olives

bay leaves

lime

smokie fillets

tomato purée

1 Melt 75 g/3 oz of the butter and place with the smokies into a food processor. Process until smooth. Add the lime rind and juice, tomato purée, whisky, breadcrumbs and pepper. Process again, until smooth.

2 Fill 4 individual ramekins with the smokie spread and press down well leaving a 1 cm/½ in space at the top. Cover and chill.

3 Melt the remaining butter and cool. Pour over each pot to fill to the top. Garnish with bay and olives. Chill until set, then cover with clear film.

Potted Cheese Rarebit

An instant 'cheese on toast' in a pot. Try using Gruyère cheese instead of the Cheddar as a variation. You may wish to serve it with a sprinkling of Worcestershire sauce or anchovy essence.

Makes 775 g/1¹/₂ lb

INGREDIENTS
50 g/2 oz/4 tbsp butter
15 ml/1 tbsp herbed French mustard
¹/₂ tsp freshly ground black pepper
100 ml/4 fl oz/¹/₂ cup ale or cider
450 g/1 lb mature Cheddar, grated

Cheddar

black pepper

French mustard

1 Place the butter, mustard, pepper and ale or cider into a saucepan. Heat gently, stirring occasionally, until boiling.

2 Add the cheese, take off the heat and stir until the cheese has melted and the mixture is creamy.

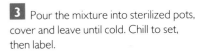

3 Pour the mixture into sterilized pots, cover and leave until cold. Chill to set, then label.

Farmhouse Pâté

This pâté is full of flavour and can be cut into slices for easy serving. You can make the pâté in 4 individual dishes, or make 1 pâté in a 450 g/1 lb container.

Makes 450 g/1 lb

INGREDIENTS
8 slices rindless streaky bacon
175 g/6 oz/2 chicken breasts
225 g/8 oz chicken livers
1 onion, chopped
1 garlic clove, crushed
½ tsp salt
½ tsp freshly ground black pepper
5 ml/1 tsp anchovy essence
5 g/1 tsp ground mace
15 g/1 tbsp chopped fresh oregano
75 g/3 oz/1 cup fresh white
   breadcrumbs
1 egg
30 ml/2 tbsp brandy
150 ml/¼ pt/⅔ cup chicken stock
10 ml/2 tsp gelatine

TO GARNISH
strips of pimento and black olives

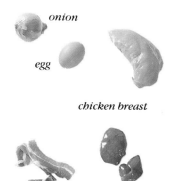

onion

egg

chicken breast

chicken livers

streaky bacon

1 Preheat the oven to 160°C/325°F/ Gas 3. Press the bacon slices flat with a knife to stretch them. Line the base and sides of each dish with bacon and neatly trim the edges.

2 Place the chicken breasts and livers, onion and garlic into a food processor. Process until smooth. Add the salt, pepper, anchovy essence, mace, oregano, breadcrumbs, egg and brandy. Process until smooth.

3 Divide the mixture between the dishes and fill to the top. Cover each with double thickness foil and stand the dishes in a roasting tin. Add enough hot water to come halfway up the side of the dishes.

4 Bake in the centre of the oven for 1 hour or until firm to touch. Release the foil to allow the steam to escape. Place a weight on the top of each dish to flatten the surface until cool.

5 Pour the juices from each dish into a measuring jug and make up to 150 ml/ ¼ pint/⅔ cup with chicken stock. Heat in a small saucepan until boiling. Blend the gelatine with 2 tbsp water and pour into the hot stock, stir until dissolved. Allow to cool thoroughly.

6 When the pâté is cold, arrange strips of pimento and black olives on the top of each. Spoon the cold gelatine mixture over the top of each and chill until set. Cover each with clear film. Store in the fridge until required.

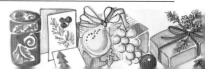

Fresh Fruit Preserve

The wonderfully fresh flavour of this fruit spread makes it a welcome gift. To vary the recipe, use a mixture of soft fruits, or other individual fruits such as strawberries or blackberries.

Makes 900 g/2 lb

INGREDIENTS
675 g/1 ½ lb/3½ cups raspberries
900 g/2 lb/4 cups caster sugar
30 ml/2 tbsp lemon juice
100 ml/4 fl oz/½ cup liquid pectin

raspberries

lemon

1 Place the raspberries in a large bowl and lightly crush with a wooden spoon. Stir in the caster sugar. Leave for 1 hour at room temperature, giving the mixture an occasional stir to dissolve the sugar.

2 Sterilize several small jars or containers, and their lids if being used. Add the lemon juice and liquid pectin to the raspberries and stir until thoroughly blended.

3 Spoon the raspberry mixture into the jars, leaving a 1 cm/½ in space at the top if the preserve is to be frozen. Cover the surface of each preserve with a waxed paper disc and cover with a lid or cellophane paper and an elastic band. Don't use a screw-topped lid if the preserve is to be frozen. Allow to cool, then label and freeze for up to 6 months, or refrigerate for up to 4 weeks.

Flavoured Oils

Any good quality oils may be flavoured with herbs, spices, peppers, olives or anchovies. They look attractive in the kitchen, as well as being ready flavoured for use in cooking or salad dressings.

Makes 300 ml/1/2 pint/1 1/4 cups of each flavour

INGREDIENTS
olive, grapeseed or almond oil

HERB OIL
sage, thyme, oregano, tarragon and
    rosemary sprigs
1 bay leaf sprig

SPICED OIL
30 g/2 tbsp whole cloves
3 mace blades
15 g/1 tbsp cardamom pods
15 g/1 tbsp coriander seeds
3 dried chillies
1 bay leaf sprig
2 lime slices
2 cinnamon sticks

MEDITERRANEAN OIL
2 mini red peppers
3 black olives
3 green olives
3 anchovy fillets
1 bay leaf sprig
strip of lemon rind

1 Have ready 3 bottles and corks which have been sterilized and are completely dry inside. Place all the fresh herb sprigs together and trim to fit inside the first bottle. Insert the short lengths first and arrange them using a long skewer, adding them stem by stem.

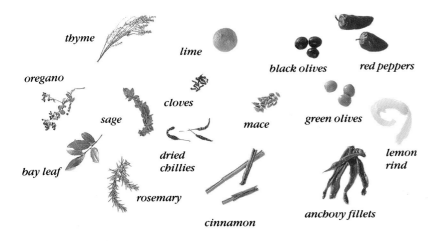

thyme

lime

oregano

black olives

red peppers

cloves

sage

mace

green olives

bay leaf

dried chillies

lemon rind

rosemary

cinnamon

anchovy fillets

2 Add the cloves, mace, cardamom pods, coriander seeds and chillies to the second bottle. Insert the sprig of bay leaves, lime slices and cinnamon sticks.

3 Grill the mini red peppers until they are tender, turning once. Add the olives, anchovies and peppers to the last bottle. Insert the bay leaf sprig and strip of lemon rind. Fill each bottle with the chosen oil and cork or cap. Label clearly and keep cool until required.

Christmas Decorating

THE CHRISTMAS HOME

These delightful suggestions for decorating
with natural materials or in country
themes will help to add the finishing touch
to any Christmas at home.

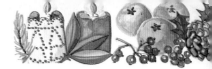

Velvet Fruits

A lavish bowl full of sumptuous apples and pears in rich, fruity-coloured velvets will look like a still-life painting. You may not be able to eat them, but these fruits feel delicious!

YOU WILL NEED
paper for templates
small amounts of dress-weight velvet
    in red, plum and green
pins
scissors
sewing machine
matching thread
polyester wadding
needle

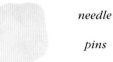

thread

dress-weight velvet

needle

pins

polyester wadding

scissors

paper

1 Trace the pear, apple and leaf templates from the back of the book and enlarge as required. Transfer to paper and cut out the templates. Pin to the velvet and cut out, adding a 5 mm (1/4 in) seam allowance all round. You will need four sections for the pear and three for the apple.

CRAFT TIP
You could also use this idea to create other velvet objects on a festive theme. Why not try making some stars or holly leaves following the other templates at the back of the book?

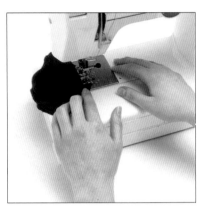

2 With right sides together, pin together the side seams and machine-stitch, leaving the top of the fruits open. Turn to the right side.

3 Cut two pieces of green velvet for each leaf. Machine-stitch together, leaving the end open, and turn to the right side. Gather the end with a needle and thread to give a realistic leaf shape.

4 Stuff each fruit with polyester wadding. Sew up the opening at the top with a needle and thread, catching in the leaf as you sew.

The Christmas Mantelpiece

In restrained tones of cream and green, this elegant arrangement concentrates on contrasting shapes and textures. Placing it in front of a mirror makes it doubly effective. The key to success is scale: use the largest-leaved ivy and the thickest candles you can find to make a really stylish design statement.

YOU WILL NEED
polystyrene balls
double-sided adhesive tape
scissors
reindeer moss
ivory candles of various heights
   and widths
foil dishes (for baking or
   take-away food)
plastic adhesive
stems of ivy
florist's wire

florist's wire

scissors

ivory candle

foil dish

double-sided adhesive tape

plastic adhesive

polystyrene ball

ivy

reindeer moss

1 To make the moss balls, cover the polystyrene shapes all over with double-sided adhesive tape.

2 Press the moss gently on to the balls, covering them well so that none of the polystyrene can be seen.

3 Arrange the candles on foil dishes to protect the mantelpiece from hot, dripping wax. Secure the candles in the dishes with pieces of plastic adhesive.

4 Wire together small bunches of ivy and attach them to a longer main stem to make a lush garland. Arrange the candles on the mantelpiece and drape the garlands in front of them. Position the moss balls around the candles.

SAFETY TIP
Never leave burning candles unattended and do not allow them to burn down to within 5 cm (2 in) of the foliage or other decoration.

Citrus Centrepiece

Perhaps because they're at their best at this time of year, oranges feature in many traditional Christmas recipes and their warm spicy smell readily evokes the festive season. A sparkling glass bowl of citrus fruits brings a flash of sunshine into the house in the depths of winter and makes a glowing, fragrant centrepiece.

CRAFT TIP

If you are using a lino-cutting tool for this project, paint the blade with a coat of clear nail varnish to prevent it discolouring the fruit.

YOU WILL NEED
oranges, lemons and limes
V-shaped lino-cutting tool or
    canelle knife
sharp knife
wire-edged ribbon
scissors
florist's stub wire
glass dish or bowl
sprigs of fresh bay leaves
secateurs

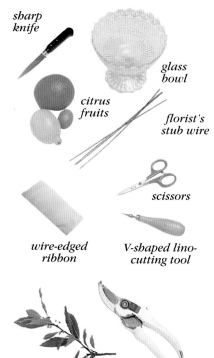

sharp knife

glass bowl

citrus fruits

florist's stub wire

scissors

wire-edged ribbon

V-shaped lino-cutting tool

fresh bay leaves

secateurs

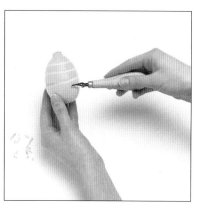

1 Use the lino-cutting tool or canelle knife to cut grooves in the peel of the fruits and reveal the white pith beneath. Follow the contours of the fruit in a spiral or make straight cuts.

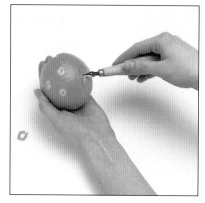

2 On other fruits, try making an overall pattern of small circles. Practise the patterns on spare fruits you intend to cook with or eat.

3 With a very sharp knife, cut thin spirals of orange peel as long as possible to drape over the arrangement.

4 Cut short lengths of wire-edged ribbon, fold into loops and secure the ends with florist's stub wire.

5 Arrange the fruits in your chosen container, tucking in the ribbon loops and adding a few sprigs of fresh green bay leaves.

Festive Wine Glasses

With the same gold glass outliner used to decorate glass ornaments, you can also transform plain, everyday wine glasses. Add clear, stained-glass colours for a jewelled effect, to give your Christmas dinner the air of a medieval feast.

YOU WILL NEED
plain wine glasses
white spirit
gold glass outliner
oil-based glass paints
fine paintbrush
old glass or jar
paper towel

gold glass outliner

paper towel

glass paint

white spirit

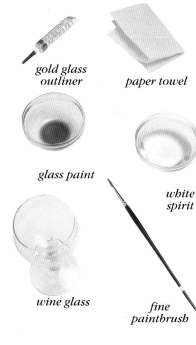

wine glass

fine paintbrush

1 Wash the glasses with detergent and wipe over with white spirit to remove all traces of grease.

2 Pipe your design directly on to the glass with the gold outliner. Leave to dry thoroughly for at least 24 hours.

CRAFT TIP

When planning your design, it's best to avoid the rim of the glass as the relief outliner will feel bumpy against the drinker's lips. The paint colours can be mixed if you wish.

3 Check the colour and get the feel of the rather viscous glass paint by practising on an old glass or jar first. Use a fine paintbrush to colour in your design, and be careful not to get paint on the gold relief. Try to finish with each colour before changing to the next one. Clean the brush with white spirit between each colour.

Heavenly Gold Star

Collect as many different kinds of gold paper as you can find to cover this sparkling star with its subtle variations of texture. It makes a lovely wall or mantelpiece decoration, and would look equally splendid at the top of the tree.

YOU WILL NEED
assorted gold paper: sweet
    wrappers, metallic crêpe paper,
    gift-wrap, etc
polystyrene star
fine wire
scissors
masking tape
PVA glue
paintbrush
gold glitter paint

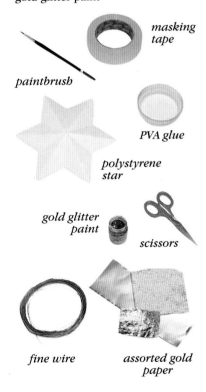

paintbrush

masking tape

PVA glue

polystyrene star

gold glitter paint

scissors

fine wire

assorted gold paper

1 Tear the various gold papers into odd shapes of slightly different sizes.

2 Dilute the PVA glue with a little water. Paint it on to the back of a piece of gold paper and stick on to the polystyrene star. Paint more glue over the piece to secure it. Work all over the front of the star, using different papers to vary the texture and colour.

3 Make a loop of wire and stick the ends into the back of the star for hanging. Secure with masking tape. Cover the back with gold paper in the same way as the front.

4 Leave to dry, then cover with a coat of gold glitter paint.

THE CHRISTMAS TREE

Inevitably the visual focus of any
Christmas event, the tree can be
transformed into something quite
magical with just a few simple touches
and flourishes and a hint of
imagination and flair.

Cookies for the Tree

Use your favourite gingerbread biscuit recipe to make some delicious edible decorations. If you'd rather they didn't all disappear from the tree before Christmas has even begun, you can dry them out completely in the oven. Either way, don't forget to make a small hole at the top of each biscuit while they're still warm so that you can hang them up.

YOU WILL NEED
rolling pin
gingerbread biscuit dough
a festive assortment of biscuit
    cutters
skewer
garden twine
scraps of homespun checked fabric

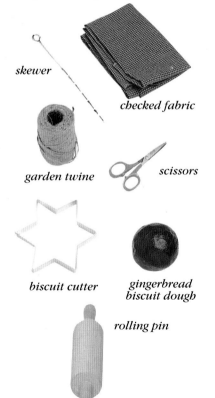

skewer

checked fabric

garden twine   *scissors*

biscuit cutter   *gingerbread
biscuit dough*

rolling pin

1 Roll out the gingerbread dough to a thickness of about 1 cm (½ in).

2 Gently cut out your chosen shapes with biscuit cutters. Bake the biscuits in batches according to the recipe.

3 While the biscuits are still warm from the oven, carefully pierce a small hole in the top of each one with a skewer. If the biscuits are not intended for eating, return them to the lowest shelf of a very low oven to allow them to dry out thoroughly.

4 Thread a loop of garden twine through each hole. Cut a small strip of homespun fabric and tie this around the loop of twine to finish the decoration.

Victorian Boots

Use the richest fabrics you can find to make these delicate boots: fine raw silks and taffetas in glowing colours are perfect. The two sides of the decoration should harmonize well.

YOU WILL NEED
thin white card
pencil
stapler
scissors
scraps of fabric
fabric glue
paintbrush
fine gold cord

scraps of fabric

fine gold cord

scissors

pencil

thin white card

paintbrush

stapler

fabric glue

1 Trace the boot template from the back of the book and transfer it on to thin card. Fold the card in two and staple the layers together at the edges so that you can cut out two exactly matching templates. Cut the boots out with scissors.

2 Separate the templates. Turn one over and glue each on to a piece of co-ordinating fabric.

3 Cut around each boot, leaving an allowance of barely 1 cm (½ in). Snip the excess fabric around all the curves and stick down firmly to the back of the card.

4 Glue a loop of cord to the back of one card for hanging, then glue the two sides of the boot together and leave to dry thoroughly.

Glitter Keys

A simple idea for transforming everyday objects into fantasy tree decorations. Once you've picked up the glitter habit, you may find you want to cover all kinds of other things – and why not?

YOU WILL NEED
old keys in various shapes and sizes
PVA glue
old paintbrush
sheets of scrap paper
coloured glitter
fine gold cord

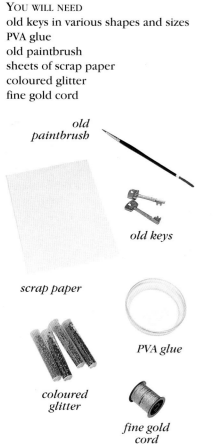

old paintbrush

scrap paper

old keys

PVA glue

coloured glitter

fine gold cord

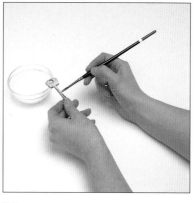

1 Using an old paintbrush, cover one side of the key with a coat of undiluted PVA glue.

2 Lay the key on a sheet of scrap paper and sprinkle generously with glitter. Repeat with the other keys, using a separate sheet of paper for each one. Allow to dry completely.

3 Remove the key. Pinch the paper to make a groove for the spare glitter to run into. Pour it back into the container. Glue the remaining areas of the keys and repeat the process. Add further layers to build up quite a thick coating. Tie a loop of gold cord to each key for hanging.

CRAFT TIP
PVA glue dries to a transparent glaze, so you can brush it on over glitter you have already applied when building up the layers on the keys.

Ornamental Keys

Gold paint and fake gems can turn a bunch of old keys into something truly wonderful – fit to unlock a fairy-tale castle or treasure chest.

YOU WILL NEED
old keys in assorted shapes and
    sizes
gold spray paint
gold braid
hot glue gun
flat-backed fake gems in
    assorted colours

gold spray paint

scissors

gold braid

old keys

flat-backed fake gems

glue gun

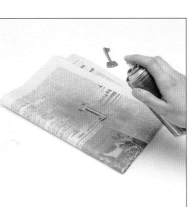

1 Make sure the keys are free of rust. Working with one side at a time, spray with gold paint and allow to dry.

2 Cut the gold braid into a suitable length for hanging the key. Fold in half and attach the ends to the key with the glue gun.

3 Cover the ends of the braid by gluing a jewel over them. Arrange two or three more jewels on the key and glue them on. Allow to dry thoroughly.

Carnival Mask

A stunning decoration inspired by the traditional costume of the masked Harlequin. Use the fragile foil from sweet wrappers for part of the design to mimic the expensive look of fine gold leaf.

YOU WILL NEED
tracing paper
thin white card
pencil
ruler
scissors
craft knife
metallic crayons in gold and lilac
glitter paint
PVA glue
glitter
foil sweet wrappers
sequins
gold doily
matt gold paper
glue-stick
fine gold cord
gold buttons

PVA glue

matt gold paper

gold doily

glitter paint

glitter brush

thin white card

metallic crayons

pencil

ruler

craft knife

fine gold cord

scissors

glue-stick　*gold button*　*sweet wrappers*

1 Trace the template from the back of the book and transfer it to thin white card. Cut out the mask shape and eye holes. Use a soft pencil to draw in the diagonals for the diamonds.

2 Decorate the diamond shapes in different colours and textures. Use metallic crayons, adding glitter paint on some for texture. Paint PVA glue on to others and sprinkle with glitter. When dry, coat thinly with more glue to fix the glitter. Cut diamonds from the sweet wrappers and glue these on last to cover any rough edges.

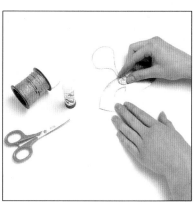

3 Trim the eye holes with rows of gold sequins and the edging cut from a gold doily.

4 Use the template to cut a second mask shape from matt gold paper. Glue this to the back of your mask. Attach a loop of fine gold cord for hanging, covering each end with a gold button.

Lacy Silver Gloves

Dainty Victorian ladies' gloves make a pretty motif for a traditional glittering tree ornament. Use translucent glass paints, which adhere well and let the foil shine through the colour.

YOU WILL NEED
tracing paper
heavy-gauge aluminium foil
masking tape
dried-out ballpoint pen
scissors
oil-based glass paints
paintbrush
fine gold cord

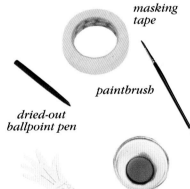

fine gold cord

scissors

heavy-gauge aluminium foil

masking tape

paintbrush

dried-out ballpoint pen

glass paints

tracing paper

1 Trace the template from the back of the book and attach the tracing to a piece of foil with masking tape. Draw over the design to transfer it to the foil. Remove the tracing and complete the embossing with an old ballpoint pen.

2 Cut out the glove, leaving a narrow border of about 2 mm ($^1/_{16}$ in) all around the edge: don't cut into the embossed outline. Make a hole in one corner of the glove with the point of the scissors.

3 Paint the design with glass paints, keeping the colours within the embossed outlines. Allow to dry completely for at least 24 hours.

4 Thread a loop of fine gold cord through the hole for hanging.

Gilded Rosettes

These flowerlike ornaments can be hung on the tree or used to decorate a sumptuously wrapped gift for someone special. Gold lamé makes an opulent setting for an ornate gilt button, but experiment with luxurious velvets too.

YOU WILL NEED
paper for template
small pieces of silk, lamé or dress-
    weight velvet
pins
scissors
matching thread
needle
fine gold cord
ornate buttons
hot glue gun

lamé and silk   *fine gold cord*

paper   *buttons*   *thread*

pins   *needle*

scissors   *hot glue gun*

1 Draw and cut out a circular template about 12 cm (5 in) in diameter, pin to a single layer of fabric and cut out (there is no need for a seam allowance).

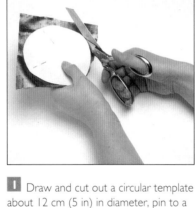

2 Using double thread, sew a running stitch all round the circle, 5 mm (¼ in) from the edge. Pull the thread taut to form the rosette and secure the ends.

3 Thread a loop of fine gold cord through the top of the rosette for hanging the decoration.

4 Using a hot glue gun, attach a button in the centre to cover the raw edges.

Exotic Ornaments

These sequinned and beaded balls look like a collection of priceless Fabergé treasures, yet they're simple and fun to make. Hang them on the tree or pile them in a dish for a show-stopping decoration.

YOU WILL NEED
silky covered polystyrene balls
paper for template
pins
gold netting
scissors
double-sided adhesive tape
gold braid
sequins in a variety of shapes
   and colours
small glass and pearl beads
brass-headed pins, 1 cm (1/2 in) long

scissors
sequins
gold netting
small beads
gold braid
paper
double-sided adhesive tape
silky covered polystyrene ball
pins
brass-headed pins

1 Measure the circumference of a ball and make a paper template to fit around it. Pin to the gold netting and cut out.

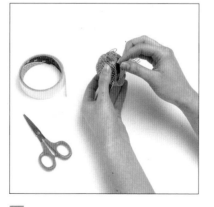

2 Secure the netting to the ball using tiny pieces of double-sided adhesive tape. The tape and raw edges will be hidden later with sequins.

3 For an alternative design, cut lengths of gold braid and pin around the ball to make a framework for your sequins.

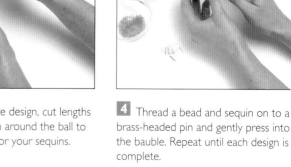

4 Thread a bead and sequin on to a brass-headed pin and gently press into the bauble. Repeat until each design is complete.

CRAFT TIP

Silk-covered balls are available as ready-made tree ornaments. When you are working out your designs, use simple repeating patterns and avoid using too many colours on each one, since this can look too busy.

A Country Angel

This endearing character, with her homespun clothes and tightly knotted hair, is bound to be a friend for many Christmases to come.

YOU WILL NEED

40 x 24 cm (16 x 10 in) piece
    natural calico
40 x 26 cm (16 x 11 in) piece
    checked cotton homespun or
    small-scale gingham
30 x 22 cm (12 x 9 in) piece blue
    and white ticking
tea
paper for templates
scissors
fabric marker pen
sewing machine
matching thread
polyester wadding
twigs
secateurs
fine permanent marker
stranded embroidery thread
    in brown
needle
garden twine
scrap of red woollen fabric
fabric stiffener
copper wire
all-purpose glue

1 Begin by washing all the fabrics to remove any chemicals. While they are still damp, soak them in tea. Don't worry if the colouring is uneven, as this adds to their rustic, aged appearance. Trace the templates for the head, dress and wings from the back of the book. Cut the head and torso out of doubled calico, leaving a 1 cm (½ in) seam allowance.

2 Machine the two body pieces right sides together, leaving the lower edge open. Clip the curves and turn to the right side. Stuff loosely with polyester wadding. Cut two twigs about 20 cm (8 in) long and stick them into the body to make the legs. Sew up the opening, securing the legs as you go.

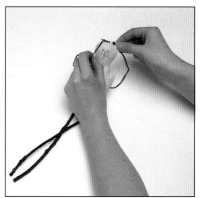

3 With a very fine permanent marker, draw the eyes, nose and mouth on to the face. Make heavy French knots with embroidery thread around the top of the face for the hair.

4 Use the paper pattern to cut out the dress from the checked fabric. Sew up the sides, leaving the sleeves and hem with raw edges. Cut a slit in the top for the neck and turn the dress to the right side. Cut a small heart from the red woollen fabric and attach to the dress with a single cross-stitch in brown embroidery thread. Put the dress on the angel, then place short twigs inside the sleeves, securing them tightly at the wrists with garden twine. The twigs should be short enough to let the arms bend forward.

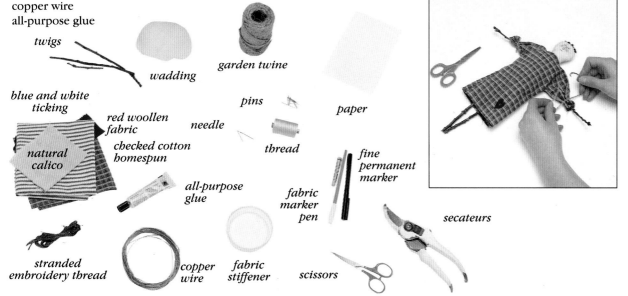

twigs

wadding

garden twine

blue and white ticking

pins

paper

red woollen fabric

needle

natural calico

checked cotton homespun

thread

fine permanent marker

all-purpose glue

fabric marker pen

secateurs

stranded embroidery thread

copper wire

fabric stiffener

scissors

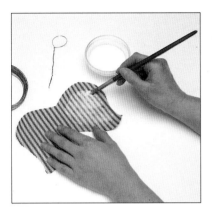

5 Cut the wings out of the ticking and fray the raw edges slightly. Apply fabric stiffener liberally to the wings to soak them thoroughly. Lay them completely flat to dry.

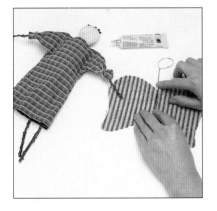

6 Make a halo from copper wire, leaving a long end to glue to the wings. Stitch the wings securely to the back of the body through the dress.

Silk Purses

Ribbons are available in a great range of widths and colours and you need only a small amount of each to make these delicate little purses to hang on your tree. Use luxurious satins or sheer organza, with contrasting colours for generous bows around the top.

YOU WILL NEED
an assortment of ribbons
pins
scissors
matching thread
needle
fine gold cord
polyester wadding

needle

thread

polyester wadding

pins

fine gold cord

scissors

ribbons

1 Cut enough ribbon to make a pleasing purse shape when folded in two, short sides together, allowing for the raw edges to be folded down at the top. To make a striped purse, pin and stitch three narrower lengths together using running stitch.

2 With the right sides together, sew up the sides of the purse by hand, or using a sewing machine if you prefer.

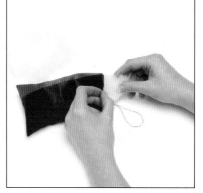

3 Turn the purse right side out and tuck the raw edges inside. Stitch on a loop of fine gold cord for hanging. Stuff lightly with polyester wadding.

4 Gather the top of the purse together and tie with another piece of ribbon, finishing with a pretty bow.

Gilded Glass Spheres

With a gold glass outliner, you can turn plain glass tree decorations into unique gilded ornaments. Don't be too ambitious with your designs: you'll find that simple repeating motifs such as circles, triangles and stars are best to begin with and can be the most effective.

YOU WILL NEED
plain glass tree ornaments
white spirit
gold glass outliner
paper tissues
jam jar
wire-edged ribbon
scissors

scissors

jam jar

plain glass tree ornament

gold glass outliner

paper tissues

wire-edged ribbon

white spirit

1 Clean the glass ornaments with detergent and wipe them with white spirit to remove all traces of grease.

2 Working on one side only, gently squeeze the gold glass outliner on to the glass in your chosen design. If you make a mistake, wipe the outliner off quickly with a paper tissue while it is still wet.

3 Rest the sphere in an empty jam jar and leave for about 24 hours to dry thoroughly. Decorate the other side and leave to dry again.

4 Thread a length of wire-edged ribbon through the top of the ornament and tie it in a bow.

NATURAL
DECORATIONS

No country Christmas is complete without
its complement of natural displays – the
wreaths, topiaries and arrangements of
organic materials that bring the smells and
textures of field, hedgerow and woodland
into the home.

Twiggy Door Wreath

Welcome seasonal guests with a door wreath that's charming in its simplicity. Just bend twigs into a heart shape and adorn the heart with variegated ivy, berries and a Christmas rose, or substitute any pure-white rose.

MATERIALS
secateurs
pliable branches, such as
 buddleia, cut from the garden
florist's wire
seagrass string
variegated trailing ivy
red berries
tree ivy
picture framer's wax gilt
 (optional)
white rose
garden twine

1 Using secateurs, cut six lengths of pliable branches about 70 cm (28 in) long. Wire three together at one end. Repeat with the other three. Cross the two bundles over at the wired end.

2 Wire the bunches together in the crossed-over position.

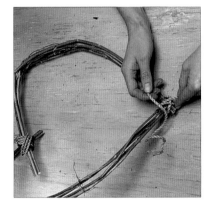

3 Holding the crossed, wired ends with one hand, ease the long end round and down very gently, so the branches don't snap. Repeat with the other side, to form a heart shape. Wire the bottom end of the heart. Bind the wiring with seagrass string at top and bottom and make a hanging loop at the top.

4 Entwine trailing ivy around the heart shape.

5 Add berries. Make a bouquet of tree-ivy leaves (if you like, gild them using picture framer's wax gilt) and a white rose. Tie the bouquet with golden twine. Wire the bouquet in position at the top of the heart.

Everlasting Christmas Tree

This delightful little tree, made from dyed, preserved oak leaves and decorated with tiny gilded cones, would make an enchanting Christmas decoration. Make several and then group them to make a centrepiece or place one at each setting.

MATERIALS
knife
bunch of dyed, dried oak leaves
florist's wire
small pine cones
picture framer's wax gilt
flowerpot, 18 cm (7 in) tall
small florist's dry foam cone
4 florist's stub wires
florist's dry foam cone about
   18 cm (7 in) tall

1 Cut the leaves off the branches and trim the stalks. Wire up bunches of about four leaves, making some branches with small leaves, some with medium-sized leaves and others with large leaves. Sort the bunches into piles.

2 Insert wires into the bottom end of each pine cone and twist the ends together. Gild each cone by rubbing on wax gilt.

3 Prepare the pot by cutting the smaller foam cone to fit the pot, adding stub-wire stakes and positioning the larger cone on to this. Attach the leaves to the cone, starting at the top with the bunches of small leaves, and working down through the medium and large leaves to make a realistic shape. Add the gilded cones to finish.

Twiggy Stars

Buy a bundle of willow twigs or, better still, hunt for them in winter woods and gardens. These pretty stars would look equally effective hanging on the tree or in a window.

YOU WILL NEED
willow twigs
secateurs
stranded embroidery thread
checked cotton fabric
scissors
natural raffia

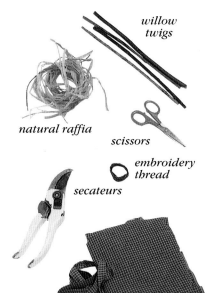

willow twigs

natural raffia

scissors

embroidery thread

secateurs

checked cotton fabric

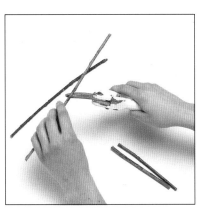

1 Cut the twigs into lengths of 15 cm (6 in) using the secateurs. You will need five for each star.

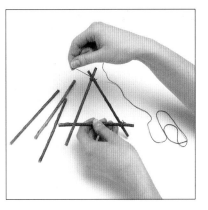

2 Tie the first pair of twigs together near the ends with a length of embroidery thread, winding it around and between to form a "V" shape. Repeat with the remaining twigs, arranging them under and over each other as shown in the photograph to form a five-pointed star.

3 Cut the fabric into strips approximately 15 × 2 cm (6 × ¾ in).

4 Tie a length of fabric in a double knot over the thread, securing each point of the star. Attach a loop of raffia to hang the decoration.

Clementine Wreath

The wreath will look spectacular hung on a door or wall, and can also be used as a table decoration with a large candle at its centre, or perhaps a cluster of smaller candles of staggered heights. The wreath is very easy to make, but it is heavy and if it is to be hung on a wall or door, be sure to fix it securely.

MATERIALS
.71 wires
27 clementines
plastic foam ring approximately
  30 cm (12 in) diameter
pyracanthus berries and foliage
ivy leaves

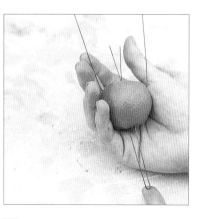

2 Soak the plastic foam ring in water. Arrange the wired clementines in a tight circle on the top of the plastic ring by pushing their four projecting wire legs into the foam. Form a second ring of clementines within the first ring.

1 Push a .71 wire across and through the base of the clementine from one side to the other, and bend the two projected ends down. Bend another .71 wire to form a hairpin shape and push the ends right through the middle of the clementine so that the bend in the wire is sitting flush with the top of the fruit. Do the same to all the clementines. Cut all the projecting wires to a length of approximately 4 cm (1½ in).

3 Cut the pyracanthus into small stems of berry clusters and foliage approximately 6 cm (2¼ in) long. Push the stems into the outer side of the plastic ring and between the two rings of clementines, making sure it is evenly distributed.

4 Cut the ivy leaves into individual stems measuring approximately 7 cm (2¾ in) in length. Push the stems of the individual leaves into the plastic ring, positioning a leaf between each clementine.

Front Door Wreath

Take a break from traditional red berries and ribbons with this fresh-looking arrangement. The vibrant orange kumquats are perfectly set off by the cool blue spruce.

YOU WILL NEED
fresh greenery: sprays of bay leaves
    and blue spruce
secateurs
florist's wire
kumquats
green chillies
pine cones
ready-made willow wreath
wire-edged ribbon
pins
scissors

pine cone   *kumquats*
green chillies

scissors

secateurs

pins   *fresh greenery*

wire-edged ribbon

willow wreath

florist's wire

1 Trim the greenery into sprigs suitable for the size of the wreath, wiring pieces together here and there to fill them out.

2 Twist a piece of wire around each stem, leaving a length to insert into the willow wreath.

3 Wire the kumquats and chillies by sticking a piece of wire through the base then bending the ends down and twisting them together. Wind a piece of wire around the base of each pine cone.

4 Attach the greenery, fruits and cones to the wreath, twisting the ends of the wires to secure them.

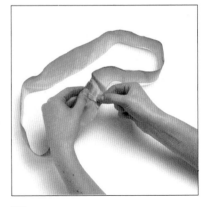

5 Reserving a short length of ribbon for the centre of the bow, join the ends together with a pin.

6 Fold the ribbon over on itself to make four loops.

7 Pinch the centre of the loops together and secure with a wire. Cover this with the remaining piece of ribbon and wire the bow to the wreath.

CHRISTMAS CANDLES

Perennially popular and nowadays
indispensable, candles furnish the purest
and warmest Christmas light – a final glow
that illuminates scenes of friendship
and love that will linger in the memory
throughout the year.

Rolled Candles

Rolled candles made from thin sheets of wax are the simplest candles to make. Wax sheets can be bought ready for use and need only to be warm and pliable before you begin.

YOU WILL NEED
sheet of beeswax
hairdryer
scalpel or craft knife
metal ruler
wick
scissors

1 To make a tapered candle, use a rectangular sheet of beeswax and warm it with a hairdryer. The short side of the sheet determines the height of the candle. Cut a narrow triangular segment off from the longest side.

2 Cut a wick that will extend about 2 cm (¾ in) above the height of the candle. Press the wick gently into the edge of this longer short side. Roll up the wax, checking that the wick is held closely from the first turn.

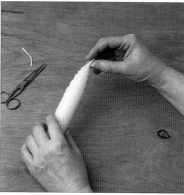

3 When you have finished rolling the wax, press the edge into the candle to give a smooth finish. Trim the wick, then wrap a tiny piece of wax around it so that it is primed and ready for burning.

Silver Crown Candle-holder

Masses of night-lights make a lovely glowing addition to your decorative scheme: dress them up for Christmas with these easy foil crowns. Make sure the candles you buy come in their own foil pots to contain the hot wax.

YOU WILL NEED
night-light
heavy-gauge aluminium foil
ruler
scissors
masking tape
dried-out ballpoint pen
glue-stick

dried-out ballpoint pen

glue-stick

masking tape

scissors

ruler

night-light

heavy-gauge aluminium foil

1 Cut a rectangle of foil to fit around the night-light and overlap by about 4 cm (1½ in). The foil should stand at least 3 cm (1¼ in) higher than the night-light.

SAFETY TIP
Candles and night-lights are a fire hazard. Never leave them burning unattended.

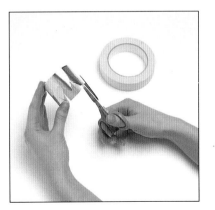

2 Wrap the foil in a circle around the candle and secure with a piece of masking tape. Cut the points of the crown freehand with scissors.

3 Remove the tape and lay the foil flat on a protected surface. Emboss a design on the foil with an old ballpoint pen, making sure that it will meet neatly when the crown is joined up.

4 Roll the finished design tightly around the night-light to get a good candle shape and stick it together finally with a glue-stick.

Stencilled Candles

Plain candles can be made to look more exciting for a party or Christmas celebration with stencils.

YOU WILL NEED
candles
tape measure
stencil card
pencil
ruler
scalpel or craft knife
spray adhesive or masking tape
non-toxic spray paints
lace or paper shelf edging

1 To make a stencil to cover the whole candle, first measure its height and circumference. Then draw your design on a piece of card to fit. Cut out the parts of the design that will form the pattern on the candle.

2 Fix the stencil firmly around the candle. Coat the back of the stencil with a light layer of a spray adhesive that allows for repositioning and stick it to the candle. Wrap the stencil tightly around the candle and then apply the paint, leave it to dry and remove the stencil.

3 An equally effective method that does not require you to make a stencil is to cut lengths of lace or paper shelf edging to fit around the candle.

Shaker Candles

Candles can be decorated with sponged patterns and motifs cut out of wax for a simple home-spun feel.

YOU WILL NEED
sponge about 2 cm (¾ in) thick
felt-tip pen
scalpel or craft knife
old baking pan
greaseproof paper
paraffin wax
double boiler
deep red wax dye
spoon or stirrer
heart-shaped biscuit cutter
plate
aquamarine water-based paint
washing-up liquid
candle
wax glue
fine paintbrush

1 On the sponge, draw one square and divide it into four small squares. Cut out half the depth of the sponge on two diagonally opposite squares.

2 Line the baking pan with grease-proof paper. Melt a small quantity of wax in the top of the double boiler and add the dye. Stir until well blended. Pour the molten wax into the lined baking pan. Tip the pan to spread out the wax evenly so that it forms a fine layer. While it is soft, use the cutter to stamp out as many hearts as you need.

3 Mix the paint with a little washing-up liquid to the consistency of double cream. Dip the sponge into the paint and then press it on to the candle to make a border. When the borders are complete, leave them to dry thoroughly.

4 Press a heart against the candle so that it becomes curved. Melt a little wax glue, paint one side of the heart with glue and then press it firmly to the candle. Add more hearts at equal intervals until the decoration is complete.

Filigree Candle Crown

Metallic candle crowns surround and protect the flames and make pinprick patterns of light through punched holes as the candles burn down inside them. You could place a group of them on a circular tray or platter, or sit single pieces on individual brass dishes or saucers, surrounding candlesticks or holders. Try experimenting with different patterns of pierced holes in straight lines and curly swirls. For further embellishment, glass nuggets and beads set into the metal take on a jewel-like quality with candle light behind them. To fix them in place, cut holes slightly smaller than the nuggets; spread glue around the holes and press on the glass or beads.

YOU WILL NEED
copper foil, .005 in thick/
  36 gauge
pencil
ruler
protective gloves (optional)
round lid or coin for template
bradawl
magazine or pile of newspaper
small pointed scissors
brass paper fasteners

1 Cut a rectangle of foil 28 cm x 16 cm (11 in x 6½ in). Use a sharp pencil and ruler to draw a line across the length of the foil, dividing it in half. Then draw parallel diagonal lines across the width of the foil, to make a lattice design. Using a round lid or a coin as a template, draw circles between the parallel lines along the top and the bottom edges.

2 Begin to punch holes, regularly spaced, along the pencilled lines, using a bradawl. Punch a single hole in the centre of each circle and triangle. If you like, place a magazine, or something similar, which will 'give' slightly and protect your work surface, underneath the foil.

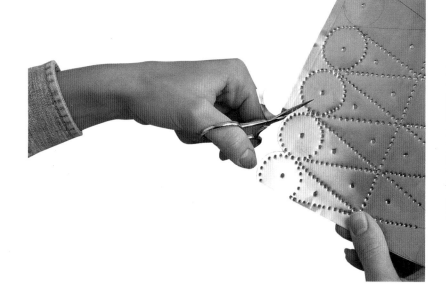

3 Cut along the top edge with scissors to leave a small border around the punched holes and make a scalloped rim.

4 Gently bend the foil round so that the ends overlap slightly, to form a cylindrical candle crown. Make three corresponding marks on both pieces of foil where they meet and punch holes through these. Push a paper fastener through each set of holes to hold the foil in place, opening out the ends of the fastener on the inside of the crown.

Painted Candlesticks

New wooden candlesticks can be aged and mellowed using simple paint techniques which instantly give a patina of age.

YOU WILL NEED
FOR THE ANTIQUE-FINISH
CANDLESTICK
wooden candlestick
wax candle
off-white emulsion paint
small, flat and fine paintbrushes
fine sandpaper or wire wool
antiquing patina
rag
acrylic paints (smoke blue and
   jade green)
matt varnish
varnishing brush

FOR THE GOLD CANDLESTICKS
candlestick
gold paint
paintbrushes
craquelure base varnish
craquelure varnish
antiquing wax or raw umber oil
   pigment
soft cotton cloth
matt varnish
varnishing brush

1 For the antique-finish candlestick, rub the candlestick with the candle, applying a light coating of wax. Paint the candlestick with off-white emulsion and leave to dry. Lightly rub over the candlestick, using fine sandpaper or wire wool, to give a scuffed surface.

2 Apply a coat of antiquing patina with a brush. Lift off some of the patina with a rag to mellow the painted surface and add texture.

3 Using a fine paintbrush, roughly paint bands of smoke blue around the top and bottom of the candlestick as well as inside any grooves. Leave to dry. Roughly paint thin lines of jade green within the smoke blue bands. Leave to dry then varnish.

1 For the gold candlestick, paint the candlestick gold, taking care not to let the paint build up in any grooves. Spread the paint with even, regular brushstrokes. Leave the paint to dry thoroughly.

2 Brush on an even coat of craquelure base varnish and let it dry. Next, use a clean, dry brush to apply an even coat of craquelure varnish to the entire surface, making sure that the base coat of varnish is thoroughly covered. Smooth out the varnish and put the candlestick aside to dry naturally (this will take about 15–20 minutes). Colourless cracks will form over the surface. Take a cotton rag and rub on a little antiquing wax or oil pigment and then seal the surface with a coat of varnish.

Advent Candle Ring

An Advent candle ring makes a pretty Christmas centrepiece. This one – decorated with glossy green tree ivy, Cape gooseberries, dried citrus-fruit slices and bundles of cinnamon sticks – is a delight to the eye, while giving off a rich seasonal aroma.

MATERIALS
florist's foam
knife
florist's ring basket
4 church candles
moss
dried orange slices
florist's stub wires
secateurs
cinnamon sticks
golden twine
tree ivy
Cape gooseberries

1 Soak the florist's foam and cut it to fit the ring basket.

2 Position the candles in the foam.

3 Cover the florist's foam with moss, pushing it well down at the sides of the basket.

4 Wire the orange slices by passing a stub wire through the centre and then twisting the ends together at the outside edge. Wire the cinnamon sticks into bundles, then tie them with golden twine and pass a wire through the string.

5 Wire the tree-ivy into bundles.

6 Position the ivy leaves into the ring. Decorate by fixing in the orange slices and cinnamon sticks and placing the Cape gooseberries on top of the candle ring at intervals.

Candle Centrepiece

Even the humblest materials can be put together to make an elegant centrepiece. The garden shed has been raided for this one, which is made from a terracotta flowerpot and chicken wire. Fill it up with red berries, ivies and white roses for a rich, Christmassy look; or substitute seasonal flowers and foliage at any other time of year.

MATERIALS
18 cm (7 in) flowerpot
about 1 m (40 in) chicken wire
knife
florist's foam ball to fit the
  diameter of the pot
beeswax candle
tree ivy
white roses
berries
variegated trailing ivy

1 Place the pot in the centre of a large square of chicken wire. Bring the chicken wire up around the pot and bend it into position.

2 Cut the florist's foam ball in half and soak one half. The other half isn't needed.

3 Place the foam in the pot, cut-side up so that you have a flat surface. Position the candle in the centre of the pot.

4 Arrange glossy tree-ivy all around the candle, to provide a lush green base.

5 Add a white rose as a focal point, and bunches of red berries among the ivy.

6 Add more white roses, and intersperse trailing variegated ivy among the tree ivy.

Gold leaf Candles

Gold leaf is expensive if you use it in large quantities but it has a special quality all of its own. It can be used to decorate candles to give stunning results. English transfer leaf – the best kind to use for this job – can be bought in books which contain several sheets. If you feel confident, you can draw designs freehand, transferring a pattern directly on to the candles. However, although the technique is very easy, mistakes can prove quite costly. If you are trying this for the first time, you should draw your design on paper before you start. The safest method is to trace a pattern on to the gold leaf.

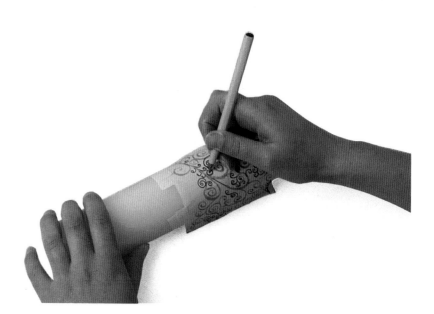

YOU WILL NEED
tracing paper
felt-tip pen
sheets of gold leaf
candle
masking tape
scissors
ballpoint pen or blunt-ended
  instrument

1 Draw your design on to tracing paper (the sheets from between the gold leaf transfer are ideal for this purpose because they match the gold leaf exactly in size).

2 Position a sheet of gold leaf transfer, gold side against the candle, and fix it firmly in place with strips of masking tape. Place the tracing paper with your design over the gold leaf. Fix it lightly in place with masking tape so that you can lift it off and reposition it later. Draw over the pattern with a ballpoint pen – there is no harm in embellishing your basic design at this stage if you want to.

3 Peel back the gold leaf transfer, checking that all the pattern has been successfully transferred. If necessary, replace it and trace parts again.

4 Using fresh sheets of gold leaf, and re-using your tracing paper design, repeat all the above until a gold pattern has been applied all over the candle. As more of the candle becomes decorated try not to stick masking tape on to areas where the pattern has already been applied.

TEMPLATES

*These templates are used in some of the projects in
the book. You can trace them direct from the page
and enlarge them to the size you want.*

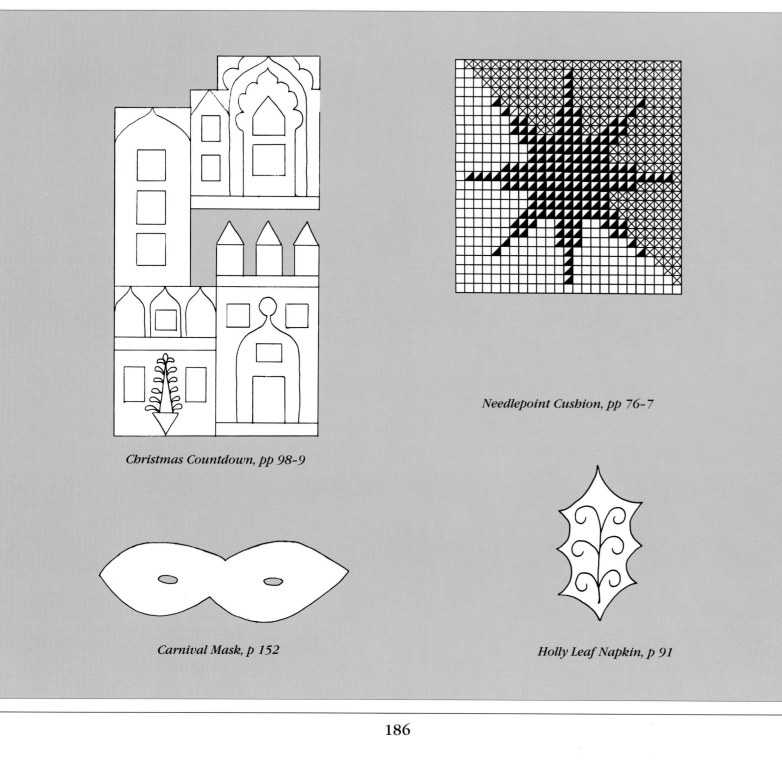

Christmas Countdown, pp 98-9

Needlepoint Cushion, pp 76-7

Carnival Mask, p 152

Holly Leaf Napkin, p 91

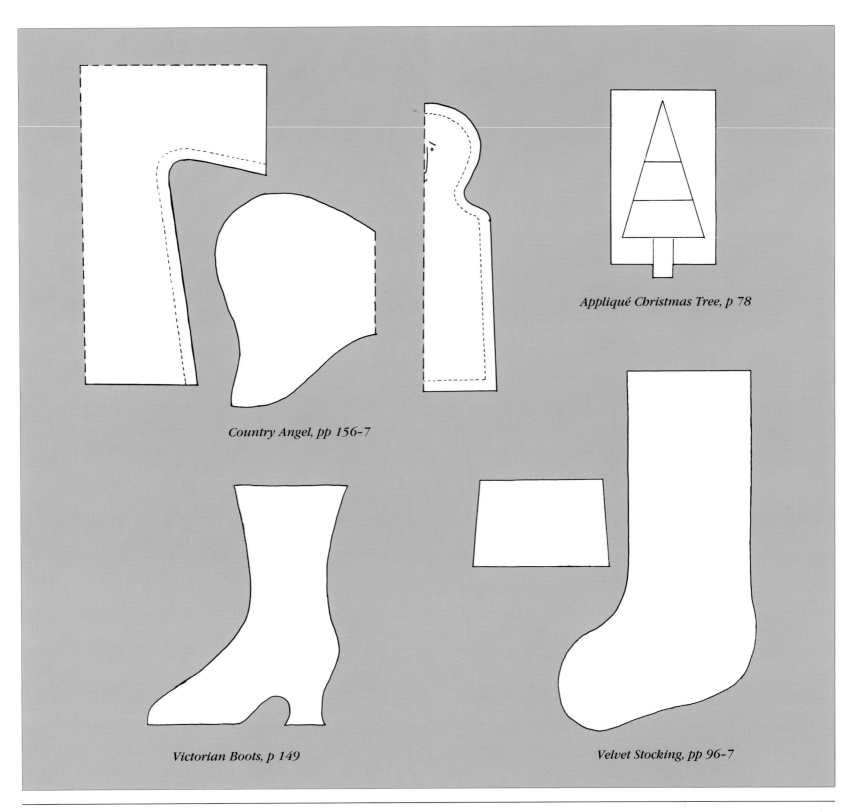

Country Angel, pp 156-7

Appliqué Christmas Tree, p 78

Victorian Boots, p 149

Velvet Stocking, pp 96-7

Lacy Silver Gloves, p 153

Gold Crown Tablecloth, p 88

Collage Gift-wrap, pp 110-11

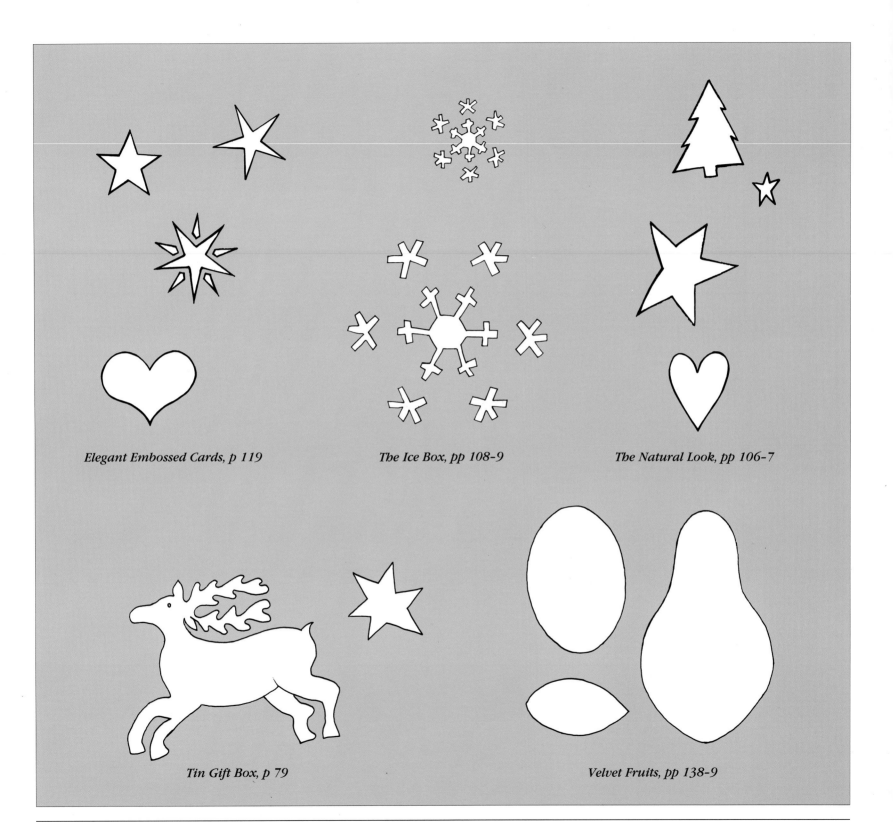

Elegant Embossed Cards, p 119

The Ice Box, pp 108–9

The Natural Look, pp 106–7

Tin Gift Box, p 79

Velvet Fruits, pp 138–9